OpenCV 3.0 Computer Vision with Java

Create multiplatform computer vision desktop and web applications using the combination of OpenCV and Java

Daniel Lélis Baggio

BIRMINGHAM - MUMBAI

OpenCV 3.0 Computer Vision with Java

First published: July 2015

Production reference: 1270715

Published by Packt Publishing Ltd.
Livery Place
35 Livery Street
Birmingham B3 2PB, UK.

ISBN 978-1-78328-397-2

www.packtpub.com

Credits

Author
Daniel Lélis Baggio

Reviewers
Ngoc Dao
Dileep Kumar Kotha
Domenico Luciani
Sebastian Montabone

Commissioning Editor
Kunal Parikh

Acquisition Editor
Harsha Bharwani

Content Development Editor
Nikhil Potdukhe

Technical Editor
Parag Topre

Copy Editors
Sarang Chari
Sonia Mathur
Swati Priya
Neha Vyas

Project Coordinator
Judie Jose

Proofreader
Safis Editing

Indexer
Monica Ajmera Mehta

Graphics
Disha Haria

Production Coordinator
Arvindkumar Gupta

Cover Work
Arvindkumar Gupta

About the Author

Daniel Lélis Baggio started his work in computer vision through medical image processing at Instituto do Coração (InCor), which is a heart institute in São Paulo, Brazil, where he worked with intravascular ultrasound (IVUS) image segmentation. After this, he focused on GPGPU and ported that algorithm to work with NVIDIA's CUDA. He also dived into the topic of six degrees of freedom (6DoF), head tracking through a project called EHCI (`http://code.google.com/p/ehci/`) with the Natural User Interface group.

He is also the author of *Mastering OpenCV with Practical Computer Vision Projects*, *Packt Publishing*.

Acknowledgment

I'd first like to thank God for all the opportunities He has given me as well as for giving me our happy family.

I'd certainly like to thank Professor Sergio Furuie for introducing me to this wonderful world of computer vision. I'd also like to thank Professor Carlos Henrique Forster for his courses on the subject.

A big thanks goes to all the reviewers of this book, who took their time to put constructive and interesting corrections to its contents.

I would also like to thank the people from Packt Publishing—especially Parag Topre, Nikhil Potdukhe, Sriram Neelakantan, Harsha Bharwani, Sageer Parkar, and Nadeem Bagban—without whom, this book would never have been finished. I would also like to thank them for their patience.

I would like to thank my parents, who brought me into this world and educated me. I also thank my brother for always being there for me.

I dedicate this book to my children, who will always be part of my heart.

I'd also like to thank my wife for supporting me day and night in our life's journey.

About the Reviewers

Ngoc Dao studied computer vision at the Computer Vision and Image Media Lab of the University of Tsukuba, Japan. He has created several high-speed and scalable image matching server systems using Scala, Akka, and MongoDB with OpenCV's Java binding. These systems can scale multiple machines and have successfully been used with many iOS and Android apps.

Other than computer vision, Ngoc is also interested in real-time distributed systems and web frameworks. He is the main author of Xitrum, which is an open source async and clustered web framework for Scala (`http://xitrum-framework.github.io`). He presented this framework at the Scala Matsuri 2014 conference in Tokyo (`http://scalamatsuri.org/en/program/index.html`).

> I would like to thank Professor Yuichi Ohta, Professor Yoshinari Kameda, and Professor Kitahara Itaru at the University of Tsukuba. They taught me a lot about computer vision.

Dileep Kumar Kotha currently works as a senior software engineer at a telecom firm in Bangalore, India. He is an undergraduate in computer science from the National Institute of Technology, Rourkela, 2012 batch. He started working on image processing during his summer internship at the prestigious IIT Kharagpur and has continued working with OpenCV on Linux machines ever since. Currently, he successfully manages a blog on OpenCV for beginners, which you can find at `http://opencvuser.blogspot.in/`.

> I would like to thank Packt Publishing for giving me the opportunity to review this book and Judie for bearing the delays in the completion of my reviews.

Domenico Luciani is a passionate 22-year-old programmer. He currently works as a software engineer for some companies and is studying computer science at the University of Palermo, Italy.

He is a computer vision enthusiast and loves security and often pentests too; he also takes part in bounty programs for many companies. He has worked with many technologies in the past, such as MongoDB, Node.js, PHP, PostgreSQL, and C. He makes many Node.js modules that he successfully publishes on the NPM website. He collaborated as a reviewer on a published BDD test using a JavaScript book. He studies the Go language (golang) just for fun.

He owns a Raspberry Pi. He loves writing code using vim and manages it with Git. He also writes tests and collaborates with various open source projects on the Web.

In his free time, he likes running and playing Parkour. You can find out more about him at `http://dlion.it`.

Sebastian Montabone is a computer engineer with a master's of science degree in computer vision. He has worked in areas, such as intelligent IP cameras for automated surveillance, data mining, 3D sensors, game development, and embedded devices.

He is the author of *Beginning Digital Image Processing: Using Free Tools for Photographers*, *Apress*. He has also written scientific articles and a computer vision video course *OpenCV Computer Vision Application Programming*, *Packt Publishing*.

You can visit his blog at `www.samontab.com`, where he shares his current projects with the world.

www.PacktPub.com

Support files, eBooks, discount offers, and more

For support files and downloads related to your book, please visit www.PacktPub.com.

Did you know that Packt offers eBook versions of every book published, with PDF and ePub files available? You can upgrade to the eBook version at www.PacktPub.com and as a print book customer, you are entitled to a discount on the eBook copy. Get in touch with us at service@packtpub.com for more details.

At www.PacktPub.com, you can also read a collection of free technical articles, sign up for a range of free newsletters and receive exclusive discounts and offers on Packt books and eBooks.

https://www2.packtpub.com/books/subscription/packtlib

Do you need instant solutions to your IT questions? PacktLib is Packt's online digital book library. Here, you can search, access, and read Packt's entire library of books.

Why subscribe?

- Fully searchable across every book published by Packt
- Copy and paste, print, and bookmark content
- On demand and accessible via a web browser

Free access for Packt account holders

If you have an account with Packt at www.PacktPub.com, you can use this to access PacktLib today and view 9 entirely free books. Simply use your login credentials for immediate access.

To all the readers, without whom this book would not have a reason for existing

Table of Contents

Preface

Living in times when self-driving vehicles are becoming a reality might trigger curious minds as to how could computers' incipient vision works. Having a face recognized for access control, getting our pictures automatically organized by a subject or person, and having characters automatically recognized from paper scans are tasks that have become common in our lives. All these aforementioned actions have been enlisted in the so-called study area of computer vision.

As a scientific discipline, the theory behind systems that can extract information from images can be described as computer vision, and it has been adopted to extract valuable measurements from medical images, as well as to help humans delineate the boundaries of important image areas in the so-called semi-automatic procedures.

In the context of providing a simple-to-use computer vision infrastructure to help people rapidly build sophisticated vision applications, an open source library was created: OpenCV. It was designed for real-time applications and is written in C++, containing several hundred computer vision algorithms.

Although OpenCV had its debut alpha release back in January 1999, it was only in February 2013 that it officially supported desktop Java through bindings. As this is one of the most popular introductory teaching languages adopted in computer science departments as well as K-12 computer-related courses, it is important to have a good reference for how to build vision apps in a Java environment.

This book covers the basic OpenCV computer vision algorithms and their integration with Java. As the Swing GUI widget toolkit is widely adopted to build GUIs in Java, in this book, you will benefit from the chapters that deal with this topic as well as come to know how to set up your development environment that deals with native code bindings. Besides, operations such as stretching, shrinking, warping, and rotating, as well as finding edges, lines, and circles are all covered through interesting and practical sample projects in this book.

As the Kinect device has become a great tool for background segmentation, we have covered it in this chapter as well.

Another hot topic that is commonly explored with computer vision is machine learning, and in this book, you will find useful information to create your own object tracker and to use OpenCV's built-in face tracker as well.

Since Java has been widely used for web applications, we have covered computer vision applications on the server side as well, explaining the details of image uploading and integration with OpenCV.

By the end of this book, you will have a solid background in how to use Java with OpenCV from setup to server side; a brief explanation of the basic computer vision topics are covered in the book. Also, you'll get the source code of several complete projects from which you can extend and add your own functionality.

What this book covers

Chapter 1, *Setting Up OpenCV for Java*, covers the setting up of a library and development environment. This chapter covers Eclipse and NetBeans IDEs, as well as explaining the Ant and Maven build tools configuration.

Chapter 2, *Handling Matrices, Files, Cameras, and GUIs*, shows how to access matrices at the pixel level as well as how to load and display images from files and web cameras. It also covers the Swing widget toolkit support and how to work with OpenCV.

Chapter 3, *Image Filters and Morphological Operators*, deals with the process of removing noise from images as well as morphological operators. It also explains image pyramids and topics such as flood fill and image thresholding.

Chapter 4, *Image Transforms*, explains important transformations to find edges, such as the Gradient and Sobel filters. Additionally, it also explains line and circle Hough transforms, which are used to identify not only straight but also radial lines. The Discrete Fourier analysis and some distance transforms are also explained in this chapter.

Chapter 5, *Object Detection Using Ada Boost and Haar Cascades*, demonstrates how to create your own classifier to find some objects, as well as how to use the famous face detection classifier.

Chapter 6, Detecting Foreground and Background Regions and Depth with a Kinect Device, explores the important problem of extracting your background. Furthermore, it explains how to use a Kinect device to retrieve depth information.

Chapter 7, OpenCV on the Server Side, explains how to set up a web server application with OpenCV.

What you need for this book

f you are a Java developer, student, researcher, or hobbyist wanting to create computer vision applications in Java then this book is for you. If you are an experienced C/C++ developer who is used to working with OpenCV, you will also find this book very useful for migrating your applications to Java.

All you need is basic knowledge of Java, with no prior understanding of computer vision required, as this book will give you clear explanations and examples of the basics.

Who this book is for

If you are a C/C++ developer, student, researcher, or hobbyist wanting to create computer vision applications in Java, then this book is for you. If you are an experienced C/C++ developer who is used to working with OpenCV, you will also find this book very useful to migrate your applications to Java.

All you need is a basic knowledge of Java. No prior understanding of computer vision is required, as this book will give you clear explanations and examples of the basics.

Conventions

In this book, you will find a number of text styles that distinguish between different kinds of information. Here are some examples of these styles and an explanation of their meaning.

Code words in text, database table names, folder names, filenames, file extensions, pathnames, dummy URLs, user input, and Twitter handles are shown as follows: "Another way to get the source code is by using the `git` tool."

A block of code is set as follows:

```
<manifest>
  <addClasspath>true</addClasspath>
  <classpathPrefix>lib/</classpathPrefix>
  <mainClass>com.mycompany.app.App</mainClass>
</manifest>
```

When we wish to draw your attention to a particular part of a code block, the relevant lines or items are set in bold:

```
imageView.addMouseListener(new MouseAdapter()
{
  public void mousePressed(MouseEvent e)
  {
    Core.circle(image,new Point(e.getX(),e.getY()),20, new
Scalar(0,0,255), 4);
    updateView(image);
  }
});
```

Any command-line input or output is written as follows:

```
sudo apt-get install build-essential cmake git libgtk2.0-dev pkg-config
libavcodec-dev libavformat-dev libswscale-dev python-dev python-numpy
libtbb2 libtbb-dev libjpeg-dev libpng-dev libtiff-dev libjasper-dev
libdc1394-22-dev ant
```

New terms and **important words** are shown in bold. Words that you see on the screen, for example, in menus or dialog boxes, appear in the text like this: " Go to **Window | Preferences**, and type classpath variables in the search box."

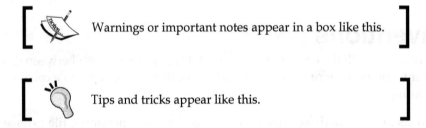

Warnings or important notes appear in a box like this.

Tips and tricks appear like this.

Reader feedback

Feedback from our readers is always welcome. Let us know what you think about this book—what you liked or disliked. Reader feedback is important for us as it helps us develop titles that you will really get the most out of.

To send us general feedback, simply e-mail feedback@packtpub.com, and mention the book's title in the subject of your message.

If there is a topic that you have expertise in and you are interested in either writing or contributing to a book, see our author guide at www.packtpub.com/authors.

Customer support

Now that you are the proud owner of a Packt book, we have a number of things to help you to get the most from your purchase.

Downloading the example code

You can download the example code files from your account at http://www.packtpub.com for all the Packt Publishing books you have purchased. If you purchased this book elsewhere, you can visit http://www.packtpub.com/support and register to have the files e-mailed directly to you.

Downloading the color images of this book

We also provide you with a PDF file that has color images of the screenshots/ diagrams used in this book. The color images will help you better understand the changes in the output. You can download this file from http://www.packtpub.com/ sites/default/files/downloads/3972OS_ColorImages.pdf.

Errata

Although we have taken every care to ensure the accuracy of our content, mistakes do happen. If you find a mistake in one of our books—maybe a mistake in the text or the code—we would be grateful if you could report this to us. By doing so, you can save other readers from frustration and help us improve subsequent versions of this book. If you find any errata, please report them by visiting http://www.packtpub.com/submit-errata, selecting your book, clicking on the **Errata Submission Form** link, and entering the details of your errata. Once your errata are verified, your submission will be accepted and the errata will be uploaded to our website or added to any list of existing errata under the Errata section of that title.

To view the previously submitted errata, go to `https://www.packtpub.com/books/content/support` and enter the name of the book in the search field. The required information will appear under the **Errata** section.

Piracy

Piracy of copyrighted material on the Internet is an ongoing problem across all media. At Packt, we take the protection of our copyright and licenses very seriously. If you come across any illegal copies of our works in any form on the Internet, please provide us with the location address or website name immediately so that we can pursue a remedy.

Please contact us at `copyright@packtpub.com` with a link to the suspected pirated material.

We appreciate your help in protecting our authors and our ability to bring you valuable content.

Questions

If you have a problem with any aspect of this book, you can contact us at `questions@packtpub.com`, and we will do our best to address the problem.

Setting Up OpenCV for Java

1

I'm sure you want to start developing astonishing computer vision applications. You must have heard of a nice C/C++ computer vision library called OpenCV to help you do so. But in case you would like to develop the applications using your knowledge of Java programming, we have good news for you. Since the release of OpenCV 2.4.4 in January 2013, Java bindings have been officially developed. So you can use them not only for desktop Java, but also for Scala development.

This chapter will set you up for OpenCV development right away. As Java developers are mostly used to working with tools such as **Eclipse**, **NetBeans**, **Apache Ant**, and **Maven**, we will cover the details of creating a simple OpenCV application using the environment that the Java developers are more used to.

In this chapter, we will do the following:

- Get OpenCV with desktop Java support
- Discuss **Java Native Interface (JNI)** details
- Configure Eclipse and NetBeans for OpenCV
- Create Apache Ant and Maven OpenCV projects

By the end of this chapter, the user should have an OpenCV for Java installation running on his OS which can easily be linked to Eclipse, NetBeans, Apache Ant, or Maven, the most used tools and building systems for Java.

Getting OpenCV for Java development

The first thing to notice when working with OpenCV for Java development is that OpenCV is a C++ library that should be compiled with operating system- specific compilers. The native code that would be generated is platform-dependent. So, the native Linux code won't run in Windows, neither will the Android native code run in OSX. This sounds very different from the bytecode generated for Java, which is executed by an interpreter in any platform. In order to get the native code running in a **Java Virtual Machine (JVM)**, one needs the so called **Java Native Interface** (JNI). This way, the native code will be required for each platform that your application is going to be run on.

It is important to understand that JNI is a native programming interface. It allows the Java code that runs inside a JVM to interoperate with the applications and libraries written in programming languages such as C, C++, and assembly. Since it bridges the gap between Java and other languages, it needs to convert datatypes from these languages, as well as to create some boilerplate code. Curious readers should refer to the gen_java.py script, located in the modules/java/generator folder, which automates most of this work. Lucky Windows users get compiled binaries, which means source C++ OpenCV code, compiled with Windows compilers into native code that runs only on Windows, from OpenCV packages. Users from other operating systems will need to build binaries from the source code, although one can make that in Windows as well. In order to download compiled binaries, we should get version 2.4.4 or higher of the OpenCV Windows package from the OpenCV SourceForge repository, which is located at http://sourceforge.net/projects/opencvlibrary/files/.

> Notice that the prebuilt files needed for Java development are located at opencv/build/java/. For instance, if you are working with version 3.0.0 OpenCV, you should see files containing the Java interface in opencv-300.jar and in the x86 and x64 native dynamic libraries, which contains the Java bindings in x86/opencv_java300.dll and x64/opencv_java300.dll.

Building OpenCV from the source code

In this section, we are mostly interested in generating all the OpenCV Java class files contained in a JAR file as well as the native dynamic library for Java OpenCV. This is a self-contained library that works with JNI and is required to run a Java OpenCV application.

In case you are working with Linux or OSX, or if you want to build from the source in Windows, then to get the latest features committed in OpenCV, you should use the source code. You can visit the OpenCV download page at http://opencv.org/downloads.html and choose the appropriate link for your distribution.

Another way to get the source code is by using the git tool. Appropriate instructions for installing it can be found at http://git-scm.com/downloads. When using git, use the following commands:

```
git clone git://github.com/Itseez/opencv.git
cd opencv
git checkout 3.0.0-rc1
mkdir build
cd build
```

These commands will access the OpenCV developers' repository and download the most updated code from branch 3.0.0-rc1, which is the release candidate for version 3.0.0.

In either method of obtaining the source code, you will need building tools in order to make binaries. The required packages are as follows:

- **CMake 2.6 or higher**: This is a cross-platform and an open source building system. You can download it from http://www.cmake.org/cmake/resources/software.html.

- **Python 2.6 or later with python-dev and python-numpy**: This is the Python language that is used to run Java building scripts. You can download Python from http://www.python.org/getit/ and download the packages from http://sourceforge.net/projects/numpy/files/NumPy.

- **C/C++ compilers**: These compilers are required to generate the native code. In Windows, you can install Microsoft Visual Studio Community or Express, which are free, from http://www.visualstudio.com/downloads/. Also, these compilers work with the Visual Studio Professional edition and the versions above 2010 should work fine. You can also make it work with MinGW, which can be downloaded from http://sourceforge.net/projects/mingw/files/Installer/. In Linux, you are advised to use the **Gnu C Compiler (GCC)** with a simple sudo apt-get install build-essential command in Ubuntu or Debian, for instance. In case you work with the Mac, you should use XCode.

- **Java Developer Kit (JDK)**: JDK is required to generate the JAR files, which will be required for every Java OpenCV program. Recommended versions begin from Oracle, JDK 6, 7, or 8, which can be downloaded from http://www.oracle.com/technetwork/java/javase/downloads/index-jsp-138363.html. Please follow the operating system-specific instructions in the link in order to install it.

- **Apache Ant**: This is a pure Java build tool. Look for binary distributions at http://ant.apache.org/bindownload.cgi. Make sure you set the ANT_HOME variable correctly as pointed out in the installation instructions at http://ant.apache.org/manual/index.html.

In order to install these software in a Linux distribution such as Ubuntu or Debian, the user should issue the following command:

```
sudo apt-get install build-essential cmake git libgtk2.0-dev pkg-config
libavcodec-dev libavformat-dev libswscale-dev python-dev python-numpy
libtbb2 libtbb-dev libjpeg-dev libpng-dev libtiff-dev libjasper-dev
libdc1394-22-dev ant
```

Once you have installed all these packages, you will be ready to build the library. Make sure you are in the build directory, as you should be, if you have followed the preceding Git instructions. In case you downloaded the source file from OpenCV downloads, the parent folder of your build should have CMakeLists.txt as well as the 3rdparty, apps, cmake, data, doc, include, modules, platforms, samples, and test folders.

CMake is a build tool and it will generate your compiler-specific solution files. You should then use your compiler to generate the binary files. Make sure you are in the build directory, as this should follow the last cd build command. If you are using Linux, run the following commands:

```
cmake -DBUILD_SHARED_LIBS=OFF
```

If you are using Windows, run the following command:

```
cmake -DBUILD_SHARED_LIBS=OFF -G "Visual Studio 10"
```

Notice that it is important to use the DBUILD_SHARED_LIBS=OFF flag, because it will instruct CMake to build OpenCV on a set of static libraries. This way, it will compile a single dynamic link library for Java without dependencies on other libraries. This makes it easier to deploy your Java projects.

 If you are using other compilers in Windows, type cmake -help and it will show all the generators available.

In case you want to use MinGW makefiles, just change the CMake command to the following command:

```
cmake -DBUILD_SHARED_LIBS=OFF -G "MinGW Makefiles"
```

One of the key points to watch for when generating project files through CMake is that `java` is one of the modules that is going to be built. You should see a screen as shown in the following screenshot:

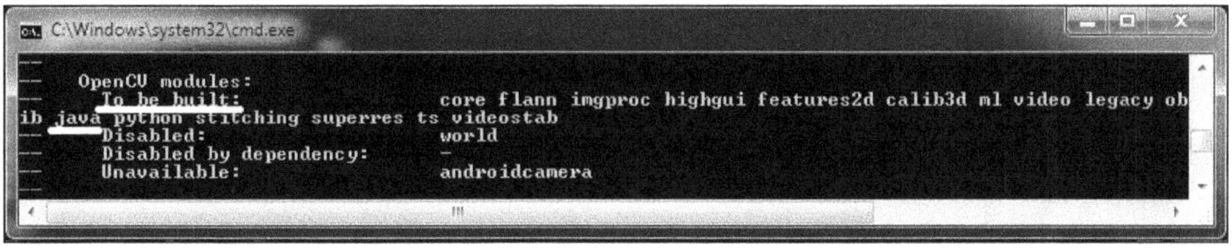

In case you can't see `java` as one of the to-be-built modules, like in the following screenshot, you should look for a couple of things, such as whether Ant is correctly configured. Also make sure that you have set the ANT_HOME environment variable and that Python is correctly configured. Check if NumPy is installed by simply typing `numpy import *` in a Python shell and check for any errors:

In case you are in doubt about the Python and Java installations, slide down to check their configurations. They should be similar to the next screenshot:

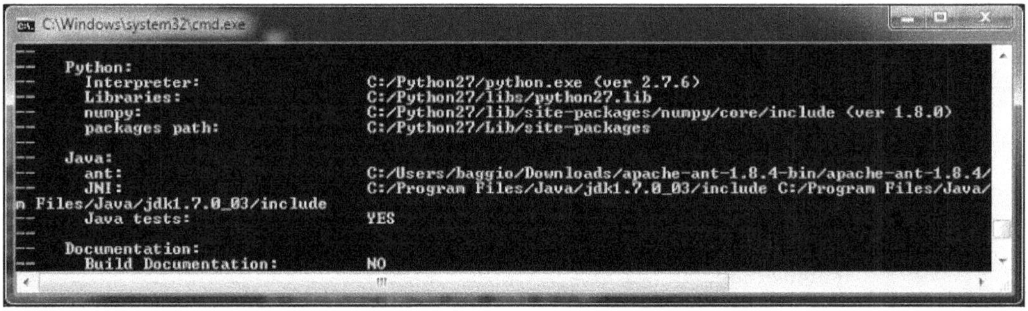

Once everything has been correctly configured, it is time to start compiling the sources. In order to do so in Windows, type the following:

```
msbuild /m OpenCV.sln /t:Build /p:Configuration=Release /v:m
```

Notice that you might get an error saying, `'msbuild' is not recognized as an internal or external command, operable program or batch file`. This occurs when you haven't set the `msbuild` path. In order to set it right, open Visual Studio and in the **Tools** menu, click **Visual Studio Command Prompt**. This will yield a fully working command prompt with access to `msbuild`. Refer to the following screenshot for clearer directions:

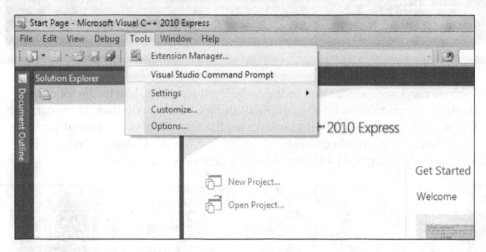

In case you are using newer Visual Studio versions, press the Windows key and type **VS2012 Command Prompt**. This should set up your environment variables.

In order to start building in Linux, simply type the following command:

```
make -j8
```

The preceding command will compile the OpenCV library with Java support. Notice that the `-j8` flag tells `make` to run in parallel with eight job threads, which makes the build theoretically faster.

Downloading the example code

You can download the example code fies from your account at `http://www.packtpub.com` for all the Packt Publishing books you have purchased. If you purchased this book elsewhere, you can visit `http://www.packtpub.com/support` and register to have the fies e-mailed directly to you.

The entire process will last for some minutes before generating a JAR file that contains the Java interfaces, which is located at `bin/opencv-300.jar`. The native dynamic link library containing Java bindings is generated at `lib/libopencv_java300.so` or `bin/Release/opencv_java300.dll`, depending on your operating system. These files will be used when we create our first OpenCV application.

> For more details on how to compile OpenCV for your platform, look for `http://docs.opencv.org/doc/tutorials/introduction/table_of_content_introduction/table_of_content_introduction.html`.

Congratulations! You are now halfway to becoming a great developer using OpenCV!

The Java OpenCV project in Eclipse

Using OpenCV in any IDE is pretty simple. It is as simple as adding OpenCV JAR, that is, `opencv-300.jar` to your classpath. But, as it relies on the native code, you need to point out the dynamic link libraries—so for Linux, .dll for Windows, and dylib for MacOsX.

1. In Eclipse, go to **File | New | Java Project**.

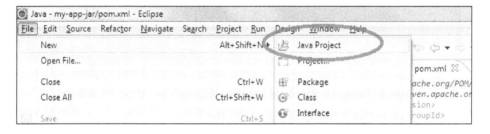

2. Give the new project a descriptive name, such as SimpleSample. Select the project in the **Package Explorer**, go to the **Project** menu and click on **Properties**. On the **Java Build Path** tab, go to the **Libraries** tab, and click on the **Add Library...** button on the right-hand side, as shown in the following screenshot:

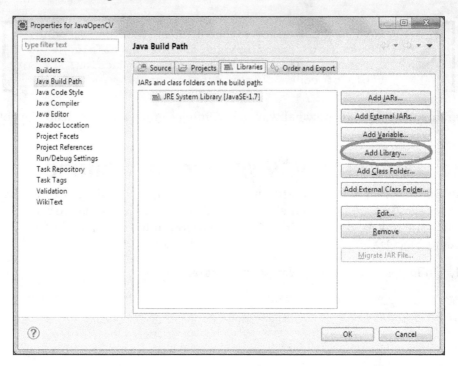

3. Select **User Library** in the **Add Library** dialog, and then click **Next**.

4. Now, click on the **User Libraries...** button.

5. Click on **New....** Name your library appropriately, for example, opencv-3.0.0. It's time to reference the JAR files.

6. Click on **Add JARs....**

7. Select the `opencv-300.jar` file in your filesystem; it should be in the `opencv\build\java` folder. Then, point to the native library location expanding your JAR as in the following screenshot:

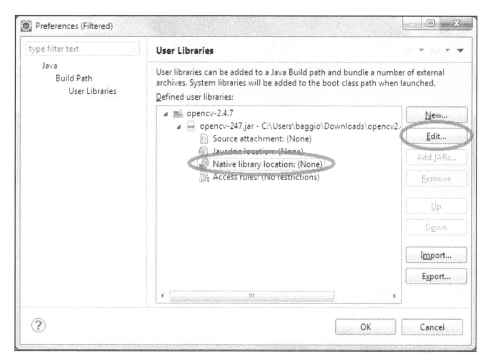

8. Now, select **Native library location** by clicking on the **Edit...** button on the right-hand side of the window and set your native libraries' location folder, for example, `opencv\build\java\x64\`.

9. Now that OpenCV is properly configured, just select it in your **Add library** dialog by pressing **Finish**.

Notice that your project now points to the OpenCV JAR. You can also browse the main classes from the **Package Explorer**, as seen in the following screenshot:

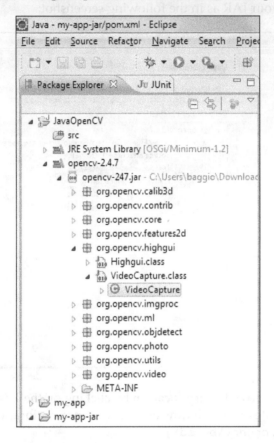

After the The *NetBeans configuration* section, a source code to create a simple OpenCV application can be found.

The NetBeans configuration

In case you are more comfortable working with NetBeans, the configuration process is pretty much like Eclipse:

1. Select **File | New Project...**. On the **Projects** tab, select **Java Application** and click on **Next**. Give the new project an appropriate name and click on **Finish**.

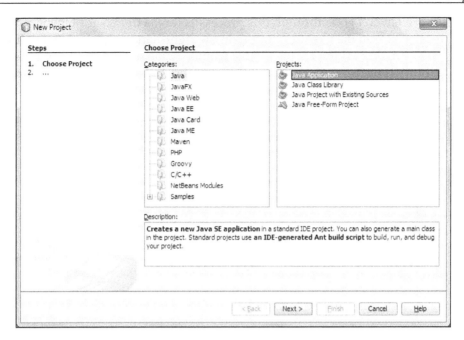

2. Now, right-click on your **Libraries** folder and click on **Add Library...**, as shown in the following screenshot:

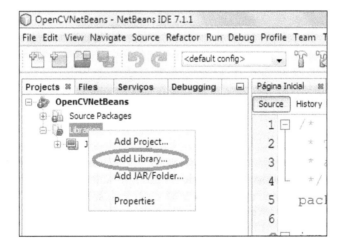

3. As we haven't gone through this process before, a library for OpenCV won't exist. Click on the **Create...** button on the right-hand side of the pane. It will open a dialog asking for the library name—name it as OpenCV—and the **Library type**, for which you should leave the default option **Class Libraries**. In the next screen, on the **Classpath** tab, click **Add JAR/Folder...** like in the next screenshot:

4. Now point to your library, which is where the opencv-300.jar file is present—usually in opencv/build/java/. As your library is properly configured, select it in the **Add Library** dialog.

5. The last detail to provide is the path for the libraries' native files. Right-click on your project name in the **Projects** tab and select **Properties**. Go to the **Run** item on the tree and under **VM Options**, set the library path by typing -Djava.library.path=C:\Users\baggio\Downloads\opencv\build\java\x64 in the text box.

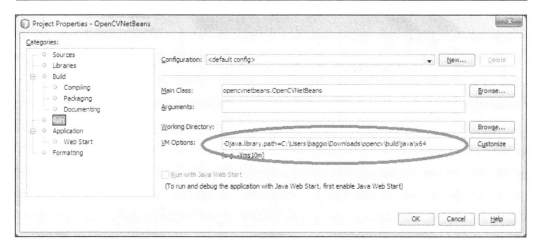

Make sure you change the given path to the one where your OpenCV installation is, and that it points to the folder where the native libraries are, that is, `opencv_java300.dll` in Windows, or `libopencv_java300.so` in Linux. Now, add the `SimpleSample` class code in your project, as pointed. Run the sample and make sure that you don't get any errors.

A Java OpenCV simple application

It's time to create a simple application that will show that we can now compile and execute Java code with OpenCV. Create a new Java class containing a `Main` method and paste the code given as follows. It simply creates a 5 x 10 OpenCV matrix, sets some of its rows and columns, and prints the result to the standard output.

Make sure you load the correct dynamic link libraries through a call to `System.loadlibrary("opencv_java300")`. Since, you might want to change the library version later, a better approach would be to use the `Core.NATIVE_LIBARAY_NAME` constant, which will output the correct library name. You can also find this file in the code repository for `chapter1` of this book, under `ant/src`.

```java
import org.opencv.core.Core;
import org.opencv.core.Mat;
import org.opencv.core.CvType;
import org.opencv.core.Scalar;

class SimpleSample {

  static{ System.loadLibrary(Core.NATIVE_LIBRARY_NAME); }

  public static void main(String[] args) {
```

```
System.out.println("Welcome to OpenCV " + Core.VERSION);
Mat m = new Mat(5, 10, CvType.CV_8UC1, new Scalar(0));
System.out.println("OpenCV Mat: " + m);
Mat mr1 = m.row(1);
mr1.setTo(new Scalar(1));
Mat mc5 = m.col(5);
mc5.setTo(new Scalar(5));
System.out.println("OpenCV Mat data:\n" + m.dump());
    }

  }
```

According to Oracle's documentation, it states that, *class can have any number of static initialization blocks. And they can appear anywhere in the class body. The runtime system guarantees that static initialization blocks are called in the order that they appear in the source code.*

You should make sure that any calls to the OpenCV library are preceded by a single `System.loadLibrary` call, in order to load the dynamic libraries. Otherwise, you will receive an `java.lang.UnsatisfiedLinkError: org.opencv.core.Mat.n_Mat(IIIDDDD)J` error. This generally occurs in a static block.

If everything goes well, you should see the following output in the console:

```
Welcome to OpenCV 3.0.0-rc1
OpenCV Mat: Mat [ 5*10*CV_8UC1, isCont=true, isSubmat=false,
nativeObj=0x2291b70, dataAddr=0x229bbd0 ]
OpenCV Mat data:
[ 0, 0, 0, 0, 0, 5, 0, 0, 0, 0;
  1, 1, 1, 1, 1, 5, 1, 1, 1, 1;
  0, 0, 0, 0, 0, 5, 0, 0, 0, 0;
  0, 0, 0, 0, 0, 5, 0, 0, 0, 0;
  0, 0, 0, 0, 0, 5, 0, 0, 0, 0]
```

Building your project with Ant

If you want to rely on Apache Ant for building instead of using an IDE, a `build.xml` file is provided in the OpenCV samples. You can find this file in this chapter's repository as well. The following are its contents:

```
<project name="SimpleSample" basedir="." default="rebuild-run">
    <property name="src.dir"     value="src"/>
    <property name="lib.dir"     value="${ocvJarDir}"/>
```

```xml
    <path id="classpath">
        <fileset dir="${lib.dir}" includes="**/*.jar"/>
    </path>
    <property name="build.dir"   value="build"/>
    <property name="classes.dir" value="${build.dir}/classes"/>
    <property name="jar.dir"     value="${build.dir}/jar"/>
    <property name="main-class"  value="${ant.project.name}"/>

    <target name="clean">
        <delete dir="${build.dir}"/>
    </target>

    <target name="compile">
        <mkdir dir="${classes.dir}"/>
        <javac includeantruntime="false" srcdir="${src.dir}"
destdir="${classes.dir}" classpathref="classpath"/>
    </target>

    <target name="jar" depends="compile">
        <mkdir dir="${jar.dir}"/>
        <jar destfile="${jar.dir}/${ant.project.name}.jar"
basedir="${classes.dir}">
            <manifest>
                <attribute name="Main-Class" value="${main-class}"/>
            </manifest>
        </jar>
    </target>

    <target name="run" depends="jar">
        <java fork="true" classname="${main-class}">
            <sysproperty key="java.library.path" path="${ocvLibDir}"/>
            <classpath>
                <path refid="classpath"/>
                <path location="${jar.dir}/${ant.project.name}.jar"/>
            </classpath>
        </java>
    </target>

    <target name="rebuild" depends="clean,jar"/>

    <target name="rebuild-run" depends="clean,run"/>

</project>
```

This is a basic `build.xml` Ant file that defines tasks such as cleaning, compiling, and packing a `.jar` file, running, rebuilding, and rebuild-running. It expects your source code to be in a sibling folder called `src`. Make sure that the `SimpleSample.java` source code provided earlier is inside this directory.

Compiling and running the project using Ant is easy. Simply type the following:

```
ant -DocvJarDir=path/to/dir/containing/opencv-300.jar -DocvLibDir=path/
to/dir/containing/opencv_java300/native/library
```

In case you have downloaded and extracted pre-built binaries, use the following command instead:

```
ant -DocvJarDir=X:\opencv3.0.0\opencv\build\java -DocvLibDir=X:\
opencv3.00\opencv\build\java\x64
```

A successful run of Ant `build.xml` will look like the following screenshot:

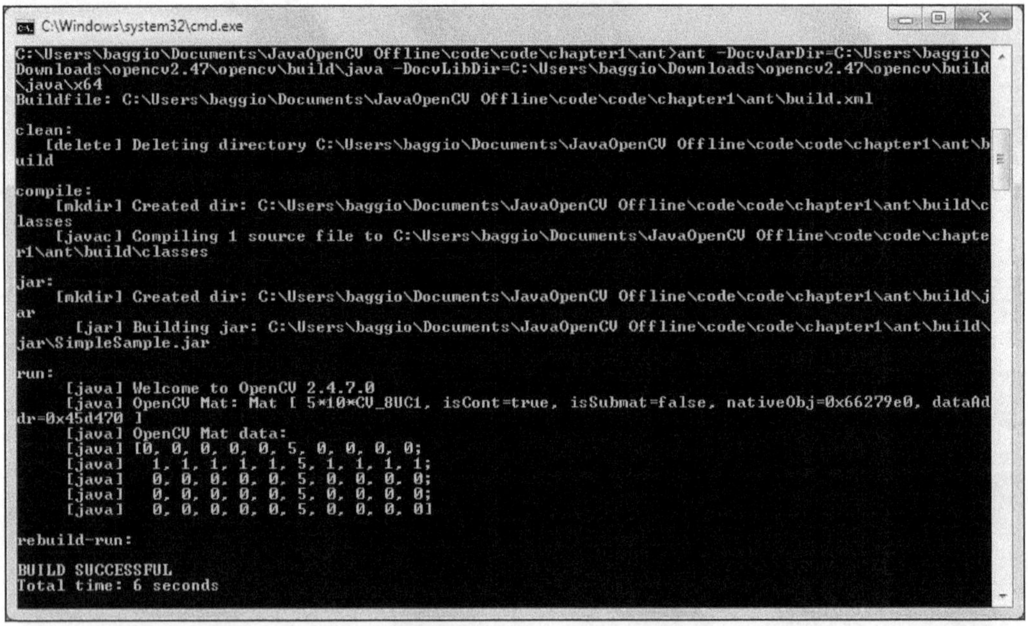

The provided `build.xml` file can be reused for building your Java OpenCV applications. In order to use it, make sure that the project name matches your main class name. If your main class is inside the `package com.your.company`, and it's called `MainOpenCV`, you should change the first line of `build.xml` from `<project name="SimpleSample" basedir="." default="rebuild-run">` to `<project name="com.your.company.MainOpenCV" basedir="." default="rebuild-run">`.

You can also hardcode the `ocvJarDir` and `ocvLibDir` properties so you won't have to type them while invoking Ant. For `ocvJarDir`, simply change the `<property name="lib.dir" value="${ocvJarDir}"/>` command to `<property name="lib.dir" value="X:\opencv2.47\opencv\build\java"/>`.

The Java OpenCV Maven configuration

Apache Maven is a more complex build automation tool, primarily used for Java projects. It describes not only how software is built, but also how it depends on other libraries. Its projects are configured through a **Project Object Model**, named `pom.xml`. Maven dependencies are usually located in Maven 2 Central Repository. In case they aren't found there, you will need to add other repositories. You can also create a local repository and add your own dependencies there. At the time of writing this book, there were no public dependencies for Java OpenCV. So we will cover not only the process of installing the Java OpenCV Maven dependencies in a local repository but also how to use this book's Maven repository for the Windows builds of OpenCV 3.0.0 version. In case OpenCV developers host public Maven repositories, minor changes will be required. You will only need to find out the official OpenCV JAR `groupId`, `artifactId`, and `version` and put them in your `pom.xml`.

In order to make your project dependent on any library, you only need to provide three fields in your `pom.xml`. They are `groupId`, `artifactId`, and `version`. The recommended way to make your project depend on libraries that are not hosted in the Central Maven Repository, is to install them using a simple command, like `mvn install:install-file -Dfile=non-maven-proj.jar -DgroupId=some.group -DartifactId=non-maven-proj -Dversion=1 -Dpackaging=jar`.

We will show you how to use the Packt repository for window builds in the next section and then we will give you the details on how to install them on your local repository, in case you need it.

Creating a Windows Java OpenCV Maven project pointing to the Packt repository

This section shows how to create a basic Maven project and how to customize it so that it adds OpenCV dependencies. Besides this, it will generate an Eclipse project so that the readers can easily generate a project in Windows. A major advantage here is that there is no need to build or download the OpenCV library manually.

Although the Maven learning curve might be a little tougher than straightaway creating your project in your favorite IDE, it pays off in the long term span. The best part of using Maven is that you won't need to install OpenCV at all since all dependencies, including native files, are automatically downloaded. We'll show you how to do it in the following simple steps:

1. **Build a project from an archetype**: Create an empty folder for your project. Let's name it as `D:\mvnopencv`. In that folder, type the following command:

   ```
   mvn archetype:generate -DgroupId=com.mycompany.app
   -DartifactId=my-opencv-app -DarchetypeArtifactId=maven-archetype-
   quickstart -DinteractiveMode=false
   ```

   Let's break it down into parts. The `mvn archetype:generate` command tells Maven to run the `generate goal` command from the archetype plugin. From the documentation, we see that `generate goal` creates a Maven project from an archetype; it asks the user to choose an archetype from the archetype catalog, and retrieves it from the remote repository. Once retrieved, it is processed to create a working Maven project. This way, we deduce that the `-DarchetypeArtifactId=maven-archetype-quickstart` parameter is the selected archetype. This will generate a Java project with the following structure:

   ```
   my-opencv-app
   |-- pom.xml
   `-- src
       |-- main
       |   `-- java
       |       `-- com
       |           `-- company
       |               `-- app
       |                   `-- App.java
       `-- test
           `-- java
               `-- com
                   `-- company
                       `-- app
                           `-- AppTest.java
   ```

    Note that the `-DgroupId=com.mycompany.app` `-DartifactId=my-opencv-app` properties will fill `pom.xml` and provide a part of the project tree.

2. **Add OpenCV dependencies**: Since this is a project generated from a general Maven archetype, we should customize it so that it will look like a Java OpenCV project. In order to do that, we will need to add our dependencies. Open the generated `pom.xml` file in `D:\mvnopencv\my-opencv-app`. We should first add the Java OpenCV dependencies. Since they don't exist in the Maven central repository at the time of writing this book, you will also need to point to an online repository. We have provided native files for Windows x86 and Windows 64-bits. In order to add the Packt Maven repository, simply add the following lines to your `pom.xml` file:

```
<project xmlns="http://maven.apache.org/POM/4.0.0"
xmlns:xsi="http://www.w3.org/2001/XMLSchema-instance"
   xsi:schemaLocation="http://maven.apache.org/POM/4.0.0 http://
maven.apache.org/maven-v4_0_0.xsd">

  <repositories>
    <repository>
      <id>javaopencvbook</id>
      <url>https://raw.github.com/JavaOpenCVBook/code/maven2/</
url>
    </repository>
  </repositories>

  <modelVersion>4.0.0</modelVersion>
...
</project>
```

Now, also add the OpenCV dependencies. In order to compile your code, you will only need to add the OpenCV JAR dependency. In case you also want to execute it, you will need the Windows natives as well. These have been packed inside `opencvjar-runtime-3.0.0-natives-windows-x86.jar` for 32-bit architectures. For 64-bit architectures, these are packed inside `opencvjar-runtime-3.0.0-natives-windows-x86_64.jar`. Near the `junit` dependencies, add the following:

```
<dependencies>
  <dependency>
    <groupId>junit</groupId>
    <artifactId>junit</artifactId>
    <version>3.8.1</version>
    <scope>test</scope>
  </dependency>
  <dependency>
    <groupId>org.javaopencvbook</groupId>
    <artifactId>opencvjar</artifactId>
    <version>3.0.0</version>
```

```
    </dependency>
    <dependency>
        <groupId>org.javaopencvbook</groupId>
        <artifactId>opencvjar-runtime</artifactId>
        <version>3.0.0</version>
        <classifier>natives-windows-x86_64</classifier>
    </dependency>
</dependencies>
```

Notice the classifier property set to opencvjar-runtime. It is set to `natives-windows-x86_64`. This is the value you should use for a 64-bit platform. In case you want it for a 32-bit platform, just use `natives-windows-x86`.

3. **Configure build plugins**: The `opencvjar-runtime` dependencies only include files such as `.dll`, `.so`, and so on. These files will be extracted to your target while executing the `mvn package` command. But, this will only happen if you add `maven-nativedependencies-plugin`. Besides, it is also important that you copy all the JAR libraries to your `/lib` folder when creating your distributable JAR. This will be dealt with by the `maven-dependency-plugin`. The last detail is to point your main class when creating a JAR, which is performed by `maven-jar-plugin`. All the build plugin configurations should be added as follows:

```
<build>
  <plugins>
    <plugin>
      <artifactId>maven-jar-plugin</artifactId>
      <version>2.4</version>
      <configuration>
        <archive>
          <manifest>
            <addClasspath>true</addClasspath>
            <classpathPrefix>lib/</classpathPrefix>
            <mainClass>com.mycompany.app.App</mainClass>
          </manifest>
        </archive>
      </configuration>
    </plugin>
    <plugin>
      <groupId>org.apache.maven.plugins</groupId>
      <artifactId>maven-dependency-plugin</artifactId>
      <version>2.1</version>
      <executions>
        <execution>
          <id>copy-dependencies</id>
          <phase>package</phase>
```

```xml
        <goals>
          <goal>copy-dependencies</goal>
        </goals>
        <configuration>
          <outputDirectory>${project.build.directory}/lib</outputDirectory>
          <overWriteReleases>false</overWriteReleases>
          <overWriteSnapshots>false</overWriteSnapshots>
          <overWriteIfNewer>true</overWriteIfNewer>
        </configuration>
      </execution>
    </executions>
  </plugin>
  <plugin>
    <groupId>com.googlecode.mavennatives</groupId>
    <artifactId>maven-nativedependencies-plugin</artifactId>
    <version>0.0.7</version>
    <executions>
      <execution>
        <id>unpacknatives</id>
        <phase>generate-resources</phase>
        <goals>
          <goal>copy</goal>
        </goals>
      </execution>
    </executions>
  </plugin>
  </plugins>
</build>
```

You can see the final pom.xml file in the chapter1/maven-sample directory in this chapter's sample code.

4. **Create a package**: Now, you should check if everything's correct by making a package. Simply type the following command:

`mvn package`

The preceding should download all the plugins and dependencies, compile your App.java file from the archetype, generate your my-opencv-app-1.0-SNAPSHOT.jar in the target folder, as well as copy all the dependent libraries to your target/lib folder; check for the junit, opencvjar, and opencvjar-runtime JARs. Also, the native libraries are extracted to the target /natives folder, so opencv_java300.dll can be found there. Your compiled classes can also be found in the target /classes folder. The other generated folders are related to your tests.

5. **Customize your code**: Now, we will change the source file to use the simple OpenCV functions. Navigate to `D:\mvnopencv\my-opencv-app\src\main\java\com\mycompany\app` and edit the `App.java` file. Simply add the following code:

```java
package com.mycompany.app;

import org.opencv.core.Core;
import org.opencv.core.Mat;
import org.opencv.core.CvType;
import org.opencv.core.Scalar;

public class App
{
  static{ System.loadLibrary(Core.NATIVE_LIBRARY_NAME); }

  public static void main(String[] args) {
    System.out.println("Welcome to OpenCV " + Core.VERSION);
    Mat m = new Mat(5, 10, CvType.CV_8UC1, new Scalar(0));
    System.out.println("OpenCV Mat: " + m);
    Mat mr1 = m.row(1);
    mr1.setTo(new Scalar(1));
    Mat mc5 = m.col(5);
    mc5.setTo(new Scalar(5));
    System.out.println("OpenCV Mat data:\n" + m.dump());
  }
}
```

It is the same code from `SimpleSample` that we just put in the `App` class. Now we just need to run it. Remember to recompile it by running the following command:

```
mvn package
```

6. **Execute your code**: Execute the generated JAR, pointing the native files in the `/native` folder through the `-Djava.library.path` property. This should be as simple as typing the following:

```
D:\mvnopencv\my-opencv-app>java    -Djava.library.path=target\
natives -jar target\my-opencv-app-1.0-SNAPSHOT.jar
```

Well done! Now you should have the same output as when running the `SimpleSample` class. In case you want to execute your project through a `.bat` file, simply type the preceding command in a file called `run.bat`, for instance, and save it in the `D:\mvnopencv\my-opencv-app` folder.

7. **Generate an Eclipse project**: Now, you will be able to take advantage of some Maven features such as creating an Eclipse project by simply typing the following command:

```
mvn eclipse:eclipse
```

In order to get the project inside Eclipse, open your workspace and then go to **File | Import...**. Then, choose **Existing Projects into Workspace**, click on **Next | Browse...** in the **Select root directory** radio button, and browse to `D:\mvnopencv\my-opencv-app`. It should recognize this folder as an Eclipse project. Then simply click on **Finish**.

In case you want to run your project now, beware that there are two warnings here. Eclipse does not recognize Maven by default. So, you will have an error telling you that `"The project cannot be built until build path errors are resolved"`, `"Unbound classpath variable: 'M2_REPO/org/javaopencvbook/opencvjar/3.0.0/opencvjar-3.0.0.jar' in project 'my-opencv-app'"`.

This error simply means that your `M2_REPO` variable isn't defined. Go to **Window | Preferences**, and type classpath variables in the search box. Selecting it in the tree will bring you the tab to define this variable. Click on **New...** and the **New Variable Entry** dialog box will appear. In the **Name** input, call it `M2_REPO` and in the **Path** input, choose **Folder...** and browse to your Maven repository. This should be located in a folder similar to `C:/Users/baggio/.m2/repository`. Click on **Ok**, and then **Ok** again in the **Preferences** dialog box. It will ask for a full rebuild. Click on **Yes**, and then the error should be gone.

If you try to run your `App.java` class by right-clicking **Run As | Java Application**, it should give you the following exception: **Exception in thread "main" java.lang. UnsatisfiedLinkError: no opencv_java300 in java.library.path**.

It only means that Eclipse hasn't found your native files. Fixing it is as easy as expanding your project and locating the **Referenced Libraries | opencvjar-3.0.0.jar**. Right-click it and choose **Properties**. Select **Native Library** at the left and in the **Location** path, click **Workspace...**, **my-opencv-app | target | natives**. Remember that this folder will only exist if you have previously run the `mvn package` command. Run the `App` class again and it should work.

Creating a Java OpenCV Maven project pointing to a local repository

The same instructions given in the previous section apply here. The only differences are that you will not need to add any additional repository to your pom.xml since they will be located in your local repository, and that you must install and create all the JARs in the Packt' repository in your machine. We assume that you have already obtained the opencv-300.jar and the native files required for your architecture, that is, if you are in Linux, you have opencv_java300.so already compiled.

In order to put your artifacts in a local repository, you must use the goal install-file from the install plugin. Firstly, you should install the opencv jar file. It should be in your build directory, in a folder that will look like D:\opencv\build\bin. In that folder, type in the following command:

```
mvn install:install-file -Dfile=opencvjar-3.0.0.jar -DgroupId=opencvjar
-DartifactId=opencvjar -Dversion=3.0.0 -Dpackaging=jar
```

Make sure you use the same groupId and artifactId when referring to it in your pom.xml dependencies. Now, in order to install the native files, almost the same procedure will be used. Instead of installing the native file itself, it is advisable to convert it to a .jar file before installation. If you are using Linux, simply create a ZIP file from the opencv_java300.so and rename it as opencv_java300.jar. In fact, a JAR file is a ZIP file that obeys some standards. After you have created your JAR file, it is time to install it in your local Maven repository. Simply type the following command:

```
mvn install:install-file -Dfile=opencvjar -runtime-natives-linux-x86.
jar -DgroupId=opencvjar -DartifactId=opencvjar-runtime -Dversion=3.0.0
-Dpackaging=jar -Dclassifier=natives-linux-x86
```

Notice the natives-linux-x86 classifier. This is important for the dependencies to specify their architecture. After typing it, you should have both the dependencies installed. Now, simply update your pom.xml file to refer to groupId opencvjar instead of org.javaopencvbook. Following the instructions from the previous section should make you ready to use Maven from your local repository.

Summary

This chapter provided several different approaches for setting up OpenCV for Java, that is, by either installing compiled binaries or compiling it from the source. It also pointed to instructions for making the main configurations in Eclipse and NetBeans IDE as well as for using building tools such as Ant and Maven. The user should be ready to easily start using OpenCV in his/her Java projects.

The next chapter will go deeper into OpenCV and address basic tasks such as handling images through matrices, reading image files, retrieving frames from a webcam, and creating nice Swing GUIs for your computer vision applications.

2
Handling Matrices, Files, Cameras, and GUIs

This chapter will enable you to perform basic operations required in computer vision, such as dealing with matrices, opening files, capturing videos from a camera, playing videos, and creating GUIs for prototype applications.

In this chapter, the following topics will be covered:

- Basic matrix manipulation
- Pixel manipulation
- How to load and display images from files
- How to capture a video from a camera
- Video playback
- Swing GUI's integration with OpenCV

By the end of this chapter, you should be able to get this computer vision application started by loading images and creating nice GUIs to manipulate them.

Basic matrix manipulation

From a computer vision background, we can see an image as a matrix of numerical values, which represents its pixels. For a gray-level image, we usually assign values ranging from 0 (black) to 255 (white) and the numbers in between show a mixture of both. These are generally 8-bit images. So, each element of the matrix refers to each pixel on the gray-level image, the number of columns refers to the image width, as well as the number of rows refers to the image's height. In order to represent a color image, we usually adopt each pixel as a combination of three basic colors: red, green, and blue. So, each pixel in the matrix is represented by a triplet of colors.

It is important to observe that with 8 bits, we get 2 to the power of eight (2^8), which is 256. So, we can represent the range from 0 to 255, which includes, respectively the values used for black and white levels in 8-bit grayscale images. Besides this, we can also represent these levels as floating points and use 0.0 for black and 1.0 for white.

OpenCV has a variety of ways to represent images, so you are able to customize the intensity level through the number of bits considering whether one wants signed, unsigned, or floating point data types, as well as the number of channels. OpenCV's convention is seen through the following expression:

```
CV_<bit_depth>{U|S|F}C(<number_of_channels>)
```

Here, U stands for unsigned, S for signed, and *F* stands for floating point. For instance, if an 8-bit unsigned single-channel image is required, the data type representation would be CV_8UC1, while a colored image represented by 32-bit floating point numbers would have the data type defined as CV_32FC3. If the number of channels is omitted, it evaluates to 1. We can see the ranges according to each bit depth and data type in the following list:

- CV_8U: These are the 8-bit unsigned integers that range from 0 to 255
- CV_8S: These are the 8-bit signed integers that range from -128 to 127
- CV_16U: These are the 16-bit unsigned integers that range from 0 to 65,535
- CV_16S: These are the 16-bit signed integers that range from -32,768 to 32,767
- CV_32S: These are the 32-bit signed integers that range from -2,147,483,648 to 2,147,483,647
- CV_32F: These are the 32-bit floating-point numbers that range from -FLT_MAX to FLT_MAX and include INF and NAN values
- CV_64F: These are the 64-bit floating-point numbers that range from -DBL_MAX to DBL_MAX and include INF and NAN values

You will generally start the project from loading an image, but it is important to know how to deal with these values. Make sure you import org.opencv.core. CvType and org.opencv.core.Mat. Several constructors are available for matrices as well, for instance:

```
Mat image2 = new Mat(480,640,CvType.CV_8UC3);
Mat image3 = new Mat(new Size(640,480), CvType.CV_8UC3);
```

Both of the preceding constructors will construct a matrix suitable to fit an image with 640 pixels of width and 480 pixels of height. Note that width is to columns as height is to rows. Also pay attention to the constructor with the Size parameter, which expects the width and height order. In case you want to check some of the matrix properties, the methods rows(), cols(), and elemSize() are available:

```
System.out.println(image2 + "rows " + image2.rows() + " cols " +
image2.cols() + " elementsize " + image2.elemSize());
```

The output of the preceding line is:

```
Mat [ 480*640*CV_8UC3, isCont=true, isSubmat=false, nativeObj=0xceeec70,
dataAddr=0xeb50090 ]rows 480 cols 640 elementsize 3
```

The isCont property tells us whether this matrix uses extra padding when representing the image, so that it can be hardware-accelerated in some platforms; however, we won't cover it in detail right now. The isSubmat property refers to fact whether this matrix was created from another matrix and also whether it refers to the data from another matrix. The nativeObj object refers to the native object address, which is a **Java Native Interface (JNI)** detail, while dataAddr points to an internal data address. The element size is measured in the number of bytes.

Another matrix constructor is the one that passes a scalar to be filled as one of its elements. The syntax for this looks like the following:

```
Mat image = new Mat(new Size(3,3), CvType.CV_8UC3, new Scalar(new
double[]{128,3,4}));
```

This constructor will initialize each element of the matrix with the triple {128, 3, 4}. A very useful way to print a matrix's contents is using the auxiliary method dump() from Mat. Its output will look similar to the following:

```
[128, 3, 4, 128, 3, 4, 128, 3, 4;
  128, 3, 4, 128, 3, 4, 128, 3, 4;
  128, 3, 4, 128, 3, 4, 128, 3, 4]
```

It is important to note that while creating the matrix with a specified size and type, it will also immediately allocate memory for its contents.

Pixel manipulation

Pixel manipulation is often required for one to access pixels in an image. There are several ways to do this and each one has its advantages and disadvantages. A straightforward method to do this is the put(row, col, value) method. For instance, in order to fill our preceding matrix with values {1, 2, 3}, we will use the following code:

```
for(int i=0;i<image.rows();i++){
  for(int j=0;j<image.cols();j++){
    image.put(i, j, new byte[]{1,2,3});
  }
}
```

 Note that in the array of bytes {1, 2, 3}, for our matrix, 1 stands for the blue channel, 2 for the green, and 3 for the red channel, as OpenCV stores its matrix internally in the **BGR (blue, green, and red)** format.

It is okay to access pixels this way for small matrices. The only problem is the overhead of JNI calls for big images. Remember that even a small 640 x 480 pixel image has 307,200 pixels and if we think about a colored image, it has 921,600 values in a matrix. Imagine that it might take around 50ms to make an overloaded call for each of the 307,200 pixels. On the other hand, if we manipulate the whole matrix on the Java side and then copy it to the native side in a single call, it will take around 13ms.

If you want to manipulate the pixels on the Java side, perform the following steps:

1. Allocate memory with the same size as the matrix in a byte array.
2. Put the image contents into that array (optional).
3. Manipulate the byte array contents.
4. Make a single put call, copying the whole byte array to the matrix.

A simple example that will iterate all image pixels and set the blue channel to zero, which means that we will set to zero every element whose modulo is 3 equals zero, that is {0, 3, 6, 9, ...}, as shown in the following piece of code:

```
public void filter(Mat image){
  int totalBytes = (int)(image.total() * image.elemSize());
  byte buffer[] = new byte[totalBytes];
  image.get(0, 0,buffer);
  for(int i=0;i<totalBytes;i++){
```

```
    if(i%3==0) buffer[i]=0;
  }
  image.put(0, 0, buffer);
}
```

First, we find out the number of bytes in the image by multiplying the total number of pixels (`image.total`) with the element size in bytes (`image.elemenSize`). Then, we build a byte array with that size. We use the `get(row, col, byte[])` method to copy the matrix contents in our recently created byte array. Then, we iterate all bytes and check the condition that refers to the blue channel (`i%3==0`). Remember that OpenCV stores colors internally as {Blue, Green, Red}. We finally make another JNI call to `image.put`, which copies the whole byte array to OpenCV's native storage. An example of this filter can be seen in the following image, which was uploaded by Mromanchenko, licensed under CC BY-SA 3.0:

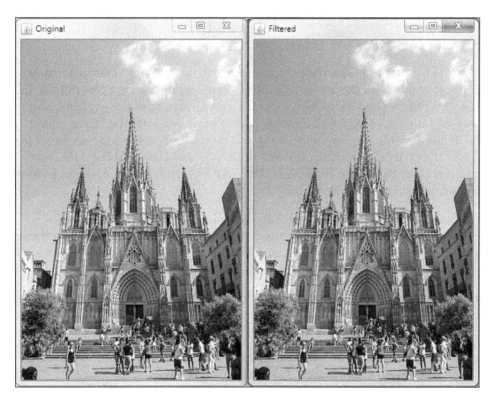

Be aware that Java does not have any unsigned byte data type, so be careful when working with it. The safe procedure is to cast it to an integer and use the And operator (`&`) with `0xff`. A simple example of this would be `int unsignedValue = myUnsignedByte & 0xff;`. Now, `unsignedValue` can be checked in the range of 0 to 255.

Loading and displaying images from files

Most computer vision applications need to retrieve images from some where. In case you need to get them from files, OpenCV comes with several image file loaders. Unfortunately, some loaders depend on codecs that sometimes aren't shipped with the operating system, which might cause them not to load. From the documentation, we see that the following files are supported with some caveats:

- **Windows bitmaps**: *.bmp, *.dib
- **JPEG files**: *.jpeg, *.jpg, *.jpe
- **JPEG 2000 files**: *.jp2
- **Portable Network Graphics**: *.png
- **Portable image format**: *.pbm, *.pgm, *.ppm
- **Sun rasters**: *.sr, *.ras
- **TIFF files**: *.tiff, *.tif

Note that Windows bitmaps, the portable image format, and sun raster formats are supported by all platforms, but the other formats depend on a few details. In Microsoft Windows and Mac OS X, OpenCV can always read the *jpeg, png,* and *tiff* formats. In Linux, OpenCV will look for codecs supplied with the OS, as stated by the documentation, so remember to *install the relevant packages (do not forget the development files, for example, "libjpeg-dev" in Debian* and Ubuntu*) to get the codec support or turn on the OPENCV_BUILD_3RDPARTY_LIBS flag in CMake,* as pointed out in imread's official documentation.

The imread method is supplied to get access to images through files. Use Imgcodecs.imread (name of the file) and check whether dataAddr() from the read image is different from zero to make sure the image has been loaded correctly, that is, the filename has been typed correctly and its format is supported.

A simple method to open a file could look like the one shown in the following code. Make sure you import org.opencv.imgcodecs.Imgcodecs and org.opencv.core. Mat:

```
public Mat openFile(String fileName) throws Exception{
   Mat newImage = Imgcodecs.imread(fileName);
     if(newImage.dataAddr()==0){
       throw new Exception ("Couldn't open file "+fileName);
     }
   return newImage;
}
```

Displaying an image with Swing

OpenCV developers are used to a simple cross-platform GUI by OpenCV, which was called as HighGUI, and a handy method called imshow. It constructs a window easily and displays an image within it, which is nice to create quick prototypes. As Java comes with a popular GUI API called **Swing**, we had better use it. Besides, no imshow method was available for Java until its 2.4.7.0 version was released. On the other hand, it is pretty simple to create such functionality. Refer to the reference code in chapter2/swing-imageshow.

Let's break down the work in to two classes: App and ImageViewer. The App class will be responsible for loading the file, while ImageViewer will display it. The application's work is simple and will only need to use Imgcodecs's imread method, which is shown as follows:

```
package org.javaopencvbook;

import java.io.File;
...
import org.opencv.imgcodecs.Imgcodecs;

public class App
{
   static{ System.loadLibrary(Core.NATIVE_LIBRARY_NAME); }

public static void main(String[] args) throws Exception {
   String filePath = "src/main/resources/images/cathedral.jpg";
   Mat newImage = Imgcodecs.imread(filePath);
   if(newImage.dataAddr()==0){
     System.out.println("Couldn't open file " + filePath);
   } else{
     ImageViewer imageViewer = new ImageViewer();
     imageViewer.show(newImage, "Loaded image");
   }
  }
}
```

Note that the App class will only read an example image file in the Mat object and it will call the ImageViewer method to display it. Now, let's see how the ImageViewer's show method works:

```
package org.javaopencvbook.util;

import java.awt.BorderLayout;
import java.awt.Dimension;
```

```java
import java.awt.Image;
import java.awt.image.BufferedImage;

import javax.swing.ImageIcon;
import javax.swing.JFrame;
import javax.swing.JLabel;
import javax.swing.JScrollPane;
import javax.swing.UIManager;
import javax.swing.UnsupportedLookAndFeelException;
import javax.swing.WindowConstants;

import org.opencv.core.Mat;
import org.opencv.imgproc.Imgproc;

public class ImageViewer {
  private JLabel imageView;

  public void show(Mat image){
    show(image, "");
  }

  public void show(Mat image,String windowName){
    setSystemLookAndFeel();

    JFrame frame = createJFrame(windowName);

        Image loadedImage = toBufferedImage(image);
        imageView.setIcon(new ImageIcon(loadedImage));

        frame.pack();
        frame.setLocationRelativeTo(null);
        frame.setVisible(true);

  }

  private JFrame createJFrame(String windowName) {
    JFrame frame = new JFrame(windowName);
    imageView = new JLabel();
    final JScrollPane imageScrollPane = new JScrollPane(imageView);
        imageScrollPane.setPreferredSize(new Dimension(640, 480));
        frame.add(imageScrollPane, BorderLayout.CENTER);
```

```
        frame.setDefaultCloseOperation(WindowConstants.EXIT_ON_CLOSE);
      return frame;
   }

  private void setSystemLookAndFeel() {
     try {
       UIManager.setLookAndFeel
(UIManager.getSystemLookAndFeelClassName());
     } catch (ClassNotFoundException e) {
       e.printStackTrace();
     } catch (InstantiationException e) {
       e.printStackTrace();
     } catch (IllegalAccessException e) {
       e.printStackTrace();
     } catch (UnsupportedLookAndFeelException e) {
       e.printStackTrace();
     }
   }


  public Image toBufferedImage(Mat matrix){
     int type = BufferedImage.TYPE_BYTE_GRAY;
     if ( matrix.channels() > 1 ) {
       type = BufferedImage.TYPE_3BYTE_BGR;
     }
     int bufferSize = matrix.channels()*matrix.cols()*matrix.rows();
     byte [] buffer = new byte[bufferSize];
     matrix.get(0,0,buffer); // get all the pixels
     BufferedImage image = new BufferedImage(matrix.cols(),matrix.
rows(), type);
     final byte[] targetPixels = ((DataBufferByte) image.getRaster().
getDataBuffer()).getData();
     System.arraycopy(buffer, 0, targetPixels, 0, buffer.length);
     return image;
   }

}
```

Pay attention to the `show` and `toBufferedImage` methods. `Show` will try to set Swing's look and feel to the default native look, which is cosmetic. Then, it will create `JFrame` with `JScrollPane` and `JLabel` inside it. It will then call `toBufferedImage`, which will convert an OpenCV Mat object to a `BufferedImage` AWT. This conversion is made through the creation of a byte array that will store matrix contents. The appropriate size is allocated through the multiplication of the number of channels by the number of columns and rows. The `matrix.get` method puts all the elements into the byte array. Finally, the image's raster data buffer is accessed through the `getDataBuffer()` and `getData()` methods. It is then filled with a fast system call to the `System.arraycopy` method. The resulting image is then assigned to `JLabel` and then it is easily displayed. Note that this method expects a matrix that is either stored as one channel's unsigned 8-bit or three channel's unsigned 8-bit. In case your image is stored as a floating point, you should convert it using the following code before calling this method, supposing that the image you need to convert is a `Mat` object called `originalImage`:

```
Mat byteImage = new Mat();
originalImage.convertTo(byteImage, CvType.CV_8UC3);
```

This way, you can call `toBufferedImage` from your converted `byteImage` property.

The image viewer can be easily installed in any Java OpenCV project and it will help you to show your images for debugging purposes. The output of this program can be seen in the next screenshot:

Capturing a video from a camera

The process of capturing frames from a webcam is very complex and it involves hardware details as well as heavy decoding or decompression algorithms. Fortunately, OpenCV has wrapped it all in a simple, yet powerful class called VideoCapture. This class not only grabs an image from a webcam, but also reads video files. In case more advanced access to a camera is required, you may want to use its specialized drivers.

You can think of a video stream as a series of pictures and you can retrieve each image in Mat and process it as you like. In order to use the VideoCapture class to capture a webcam stream, you need to instantiate it using the VideoCapture(int device) constructor. Note that the constructor parameter refers to the camera index in case you have several cameras. So, if you have one built-in camera and one USB camera and you create a videocapture object, such as new VideoCapture(1), then this object will refer to your built-in camera, while new VideoCapture(0) will refer to your just-plugged-in USB camera or the other way around. Make sure the cameras work in a manufacturer test application and check whether the camera's drivers are also installed before you try to capture images in OpenCV.

After instantiating your VideoCapture class, check whether it is instantiated with the isOpened() method. This will be false in case something went wrong while accessing your camera. Unfortunately, there won't be much more info, so double-check your drivers. Now that everything is working, call the read() method to retrieve each captured frame in a loop. Note that this method combines the VideoCapture grab() and retrieve() methods. The grab() method only captures the next frame, which is fast, while the retrieve() method decodes and returns the captured frame. These methods make more sense when synchronization is important or when you use several cameras, as it will be easier to capture frames that are as close as possible, firstly by calling grab() for all cameras and then calling retrieve(). In case things go wrong while using the read() method, that is, the camera gets disconnected, then the method returns false.

Another important point that you need to remember when using the VideoCapture class is setting the desired camera resolution. This is possible through the set() property setting method, which requires the Videoio.CAP_PROP_FRAME_WIDTH and Videoio.CAP_PROP_FRAME_WIDTH parameters. In case you want a 640 x 480 resolution, you would have to make two calls, as follows:

```
VideoCapture capture = new VideoCapture(0);
capture.set(Videoio.CAP_PROP_FRAME_WIDTH,640);
capture.set(Videoio.CAP_PROP_FRAME_HEIGHT,480);
```

Before attempting to set the new resolutions, check your device's capabilities. If you set a resolution the camera can't handle, this might hang the camera or fallback to a resolution where it can capture an image.

The videocapture project available in this chapter's sample code shows how to retrieve a webcam stream and display it in the screen pretty much like what happens in the previous swing-imageshow example. In this project, the toBufferedImage method has been refactored to an ImageProcessor class, which deals only with the conversion from Mat — retrieved from the VideoCapture class — to BufferedImage, which is required to display the image in Swing. The main class is also very simple; it only builds a window, instantiates a VideoCapture class, sets its properties, and goes to a main loop. This will grab a frame from the camera, convert it to BufferedImage and display it in JLabel, as shown in the following code:

```java
package org.javaopencvbook;

import java.awt.Image;
import java.io.File;

import javax.swing.ImageIcon;
import javax.swing.JFrame;
import javax.swing.JLabel;

import org.javaopencvbook.utils.ImageProcessor;
import org.opencv.core.Core;
import org.opencv.core.Mat;
import org.opencv.videoio.Videoio;
import org.opencv.videoio.VideoCapture;

public class App
{
    static{ System.loadLibrary(Core.NATIVE_LIBRARY_NAME);
    }

    private JFrame frame;
    private JLabel imageLabel;

    public static void main(String[] args) {
        App app = new App();
        app.initGUI();
        app.runMainLoop(args);
    }

    private void initGUI() {
```

```
      frame = new JFrame("Camera Input Example");
      frame.setDefaultCloseOperation(JFrame.EXIT_ON_CLOSE);
      frame.setSize(400,400);
      imageLabel = new JLabel();
      frame.add(imageLabel);
      frame.setVisible(true);
   }

   private void runMainLoop(String[] args) {
      ImageProcessor imageProcessor = new ImageProcessor();
      Mat webcamMatImage = new Mat();
      Image tempImage;
      VideoCapture capture = new VideoCapture(0);
      capture.set(Videoio.CAP_PROP_FRAME_WIDTH,320);
      capture.set(Videoio.CAP_PROP_FRAME_HEIGHT,240);

      if( capture.isOpened()){
      while (true){
      capture.read(webcamMatImage);
      if( !webcamMatImage.empty() ){
   tempImage= imageProcessor.toBufferedImage(webcamMatImage);
   ImageIcon imageIcon = new ImageIcon(tempImage, "Captured video");
   imageLabel.setIcon(imageIcon);
   frame.pack();   //this will resize the window to fit the image
         }
      else{
        System.out.println(" -- Frame not captured -- Break!");
        break;
      }
   }
   }
   else{
     System.out.println("Couldn't open capture.");
   }
   }
}
```

Note that calling `frame.pack()` will realize the captured frame size and fit the window according to it. The following screenshot shows a successful execution of the preceding code:

Be aware that when you open a `VideoCapture` device, it might not release the process gracefully, so your Java application might still be running when you close it. You might need to kill your process (according to your platform) as a last resort. In Windows, this is as easy as opening the Task Manager, which you can open by pressing *CTRL + ALT + DEL* and locating your Java process. To do this, OS X users need to press *CMD + ALT + ESC*, while Linux users can just issue a `kill` command. For troubleshooting, if you are having problems starting your capture device after using it for a while, reconnecting your USB plug can make it work.

Video playback

Another important I/O task in computer vision is being able to open and process a video file. Fortunately, OpenCV can easily deal with videos through the `VideoCapture` class. Instead of constructing it with a device number, as was done previously, we need to create it with the file path. We can also use the empty constructor and make the `open(String filename)` method responsible for pointing to the file.

The `videoplayback` project available in the chapter's source code has the same structure as the `swing-imageshow` project, explained previously. It only differs when you initialize the `VideoCapture` instance:

```
VideoCapture capture = new VideoCapture("src/main/resources/videos/
tree.avi");
```

We have also put a 50ms delay between each frame so that the whole video doesn't play too fast. There is also code that you can use to manipulate `InterruptedException`. Note that the video files won't play with the same velocity as seen in a video player device. This is because the `capture.read(webcamMatImage);` method is called as quickly as possible. You can also add delays to the code so that it plays slower than the usual pace. Although it is not covered in this section, the `get` method from the `VideoCapture` class when called with the `CV_CAP_PROP_FPS` parameter should return the video frames per second, so that you can play it in the original frame rate.

In case your video is not loaded, it might be an uninstalled codec issue. Try installing it or looking for other codecs so that this bug is finished. Another option to do this is to use tools to convert your video to supported codecs. It might also be the case where the `opencv_ffmpeg300` dynamic link library goes missing from your path environmental variable. Try copying it to your project home folder or adding it to your path variable. That should work. Make sure you point your java.library.path to the folder that contains this library, in the same way you configured your projects to find native OpenCV libraries, as described in *Chapter 1, Setting Up OpenCV for Java*.

Swing GUI's integration with OpenCV

It is important to have rich graphical user interfaces while debugging or experimenting with computer vision projects, since some tasks might require a lot of tuning. This way, dealing with sliders, buttons, labels, and mouse events should be in the backpack of any computer vision researcher. Thankfully, you can work with all of these components in a relatively easy way in Swing. In this section, we will cover the most important parts of creating an application that loads an image and blurs it at several levels through a slider. This application also makes use of mouse events to highlight details in the image as well as a nice button to click and clear everything. The next screenshot gives us a good idea of how the application works. The code can be found in the `opencv-gui` project within the code bundle for this book.

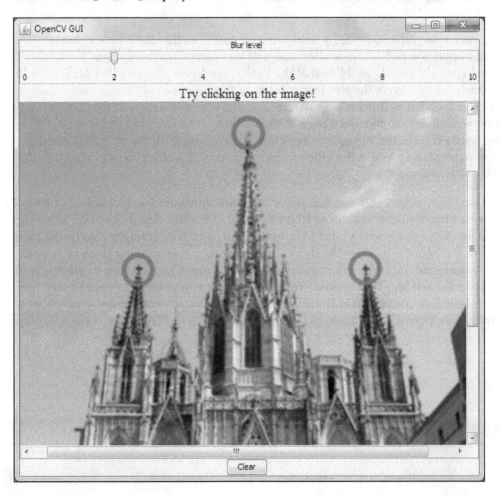

The code to load an image is not new to us and can be found in the *Displaying an image with Swing* section. We will pay closer attention to the setupSlider(), setupImage(), and setupButton() methods. Read the setupSlider method and we will then cover it in detail later:

```
private void setupSlider(JFrame frame) {
JLabel sliderLabel = new JLabel("Blur level", JLabel.CENTER);
sliderLabel.setAlignmentX(Component.CENTER_ALIGNMENT);

int minimum = 0;
int maximum = 10;
int initial =0;
JSlider levelSlider = new JSlider(JSlider.HORIZONTAL,
minimum, maximum, initial);

levelSlider.setMajorTickSpacing(2);
levelSlider.setMinorTickSpacing(1);
levelSlider.setPaintTicks(true);
levelSlider.setPaintLabels(true);
levelSlider.addChangeListener(new ChangeListener() {

  public void stateChanged(ChangeEvent e) {
    JSlider source = (JSlider)e.getSource();
    int level = (int)source.getValue();
    Mat output = imageProcessor.blur(image, level);
    updateView(output);
    }
  });
frame.add(sliderLabel);
frame.add(levelSlider);
}
```

Note that a slider is simply a Jslider class and we need to set its minimum, maximum, and initial values through the constructor. We also set whether it's a vertical or horizontal slider. Some cosmetic details, such as the major and minor tick spacing and whether to paint or not labels and ticks are also set. A key method in the slider is its stateChanged listener provided by the anonymous class, which implements the ChangeListener interface. This is basically what happens when the user changes the slider. In our case, we will blur the image the number of times set by the slider. This is done through our implemented ImageProcessor class, which basically calls the Imgproc blur method, a very simple filter that only calculates the mean of a number of neighbor pixels. The value addressed by the slider is obtained through a call to source.getValue().

Another important task is being responsive to the mouse click events. This is achieved by adding MouseListener to our JLabel image view. The following is the setupImage method:

```
private void setupImage(JFrame frame) {
  JLabel mouseWarning = new JLabel("Try clicking on the image!",
JLabel.CENTER);
  mouseWarning .setAlignmentX(Component.CENTER_ALIGNMENT);
  mouseWarning.setFont(new Font("Serif", Font.PLAIN, 18));
  frame.add(mouseWarning);

  imageView = new JLabel();

  final JScrollPane imageScrollPane = new JScrollPane(imageView);
  imageScrollPane.setPreferredSize(new Dimension(640, 480));

  imageView.addMouseListener(new MouseAdapter()
  {
    public void mousePressed(MouseEvent e)
    {
      Imgproc.circle(image,new Point(e.getX(),e.getY()),20, new
Scalar(0,0,255), 4);
      updateView(image);
    }
  });

  frame.add(imageScrollPane);
}
```

The mousePressed() method implemented in the preceding code is responsible for answering all the mousedown events. We can get local coordinates through the getX() and getY() event methods. Note that we call Imgproc.circle, which is an OpenCV function that will draw a circle in the desired matrix, in the desired position, and we can define its radius, color, and thickness.

The last GUI component explored in this example is a button that is created through the JButton component, which implements the actionPerformed interface. As we have previously stored the original image, it's easy to clear the image by just copying the original one back:

```
private void setupButton(JFrame frame) {
  JButton clearButton = new JButton("Clear");
  clearButton.addActionListener(new ActionListener() {

  public void actionPerformed(ActionEvent event) {
```

```
        image = originalImage.clone();
        updateView(originalImage);
    }
});
clearButton.setAlignmentX(Component.CENTER_ALIGNMENT);
frame.add(clearButton);
}
```

Summary

Wow! A lot of details have been covered in this chapter, but we have finally grasped the development of a complete application for computer vision. We touched on the topic of core structure from OpenCV, which is the `Mat` class for basic pixel manipulation, and its close relation to Swing's `BufferedImage` class. Besides this, we covered important tasks such as opening image files and displaying them in a Swing application. The important area of live video streaming has been covered with the `VideoCapture` class, which shows you how to obtain frames from a webcam as well as from video files. Finally, we created a rich graphical user interface application with sliders, labels, buttons and by handling mouse events in Java.

The foundations of working with a Java OpenCV API have been set and we are ready to go on to the next chapter, which will deal with core operators in image processing, such as smoothing filters to remove noise, using morphological operators to isolate elements, using bucket fill for segmentation, image pyramids, and the essential task of thresholding. Be sure to check them out.

3
Image Filters and Morphological Operators

After learning the basics of setting up OpenCV for Java and dealing with a graphical user interface, it is time to explore some of the core operators in image processing. Some of them come from signal processing and we call them filters, as they usually help you to get away with noise from images. It is important to know that several digital filters have their optical counterparts. Other operators play a useful role when dealing with binary images, such as the morphological operators, which will help you to isolate regions or glue some of them together. We will also cover, in detail, the famous **bucket fill tool**, which is very useful in segmentation. When dealing with large images, it is important to know how image pyramids can help you decrease your image size without losing important information and by achieving performance. We will finish this chapter with one of the simplest and most useful techniques for segmentation, which is applying a threshold to separate regions as well as studying a dynamic threshold that will not suffer much from lighting problems.

In this chapter, we will cover:

- Smoothing
- Morphological operators
- Flood filling
- Image pyramids
- Thresholding

By the end of this chapter, you will be able to perform several filtering procedures over an image, such as removing noise, growing, shrinking and filling some areas, as well as deciding whether some pixels fit or not in accordance with a given criteria.

Smoothing

Just like in one-dimensional signals, we are always susceptible to receiving some noise in our images and we generally apply some preprocessing filters to them before we perform our main work on the images. We can consider noise as a random variation of color or brightness information that is not present in the imaged object, which can take place undesirably due to a sensor and circuitry of a digital camera or scanner. This section uses the ideas of low-pass filter kernels to smoothen our images. These filters remove high frequency content, such as edges and noises, although some techniques allow edges not to be blurred. We will cover the four main image filters available in OpenCV: averaging, Gaussian, median filtering, and bilateral filtering.

> **2D Kernel Convolution** is a form of mathematical convolution. An output image is calculated by sweeping each of the pixels of a given image and applying a kernel operator to them, yielding an output pixel for each resulting operation. For instance, the kernel operator can be a 3 x 3 matrix of 1s divided by 9. This way, each output pixel will be the average value of the 9 neighbor pixels for each pixel in the input image, yielding an average output image.

Averaging

Most of the blurring techniques will use a 2D kernel convolution to filter images. The simplest idea is to have a 3 x 3 kernel that has a total of 9 pixels. Suppose we want to have the average value of 9 pixels, we will only need to add them and divide by 9. This is accomplished by the convolution with the following kernel:

$$\frac{1}{9}\begin{bmatrix} 1 & 1 & 1 \\ 1 & 1 & 1 \\ 1 & 1 & 1 \end{bmatrix}$$

In order to apply this transformation, we will use Imgproc's `blur` function. Its syntax is as follows:

```
public static void blur(Mat src, Mat dst, Size ksize)
```

The parameters are, simply, the source image, destination, and the kernel size, which is as simple as `new Size(3.0, 3.0)` for our 3 x 3 kernel. You can optionally add the `Point` anchor parameter, shown as follows:

```
public static void blur(Mat src, Mat dst, Size ksize, Point anchor,
int borderType)
```

The preceding line will let you position the anchor as well as an `int borderType` integer variable outside the center point. This `borderType` parameter lets you define how you want the behavior when part of the kernel is inside and outside the image. Note that in the first row, the preceding kernel will look for values that will be on top of the row, so OpenCV will need to extrapolate them. There are a few options available to extrapolate borders. From the documentation, we have the following types of borders, all available from `Core` constants, for instance: `Core.BORDER_REPLICATE`. For example, consider | as one of the image borders and `abcdefgh` as pixel values:

```
BORDER_REPLICATE:      aaaaaa|abcdefgh|hhhhhhh
BORDER_REFLECT:        fedcba|abcdefgh|hgfedcb
BORDER_REFLECT_101:    gfedcb|abcdefgh|gfedcba
BORDER_WRAP:           cdefgh|abcdefgh|abcdefg
BORDER_CONSTANT:       000000|abcdefgh|0000000
```

The default value is `Core.BORDER_DEFAULT` that maps to `Core.BORDER_REFLECT_101`. For more information on how to use this function, look for the source code of this chapter's `imageFilter` project. The following is a screenshot of the main application, which lets you try out each of these filters:

Note that this application also provides some simple Gaussian noise, whose probability density function is equal to that of the normal distribution, to see the benefits of each filter.

Gaussian

The idea behind Gaussian is the same as average filtering except for the fact that instead of using the same weight for each of the pixels, a two-dimensional Gaussian function is used for the kernel that gives the highest weightage to the pixel in the center. The following graph displays the behavior of a 2D Gaussian curve:

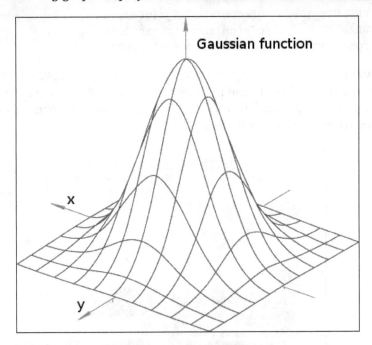

In order to use this function, employ the following basic signature:

```
public static void GaussianBlur(Mat src,
                                Mat dst,
                                Size ksize,
                                double sigmaX [, double sigmaY])
```

The `Mat src` and `Mat dst` parameters are straightforward since they describe the input and output images. The `Size ksize` parameter describes the kernel's width and height. Hence, if you want to set its size, this parameter must be positive and odd, so that the kernel can be symmetrical and have a center. In case you set the parameter to zero, the size will be calculated from `double sigmaX`. Sigma is its standard deviation, which is roughly *half width at half max* of the Gaussian value, which means that it is half the width of the Gaussian value when its height is half the highest Gaussian value. Optionally, you can also provide the fifth parameter as `sigmaY`, which is the standard deviation for the *y* axis. In case you don't use this parameter, `sigmaY` will be equal to `sigmaX`. Also, if both `sigmaX`, and `sigmaY` are zero, they are computed from the kernel's width and height. The `getGaussianKernel` function returns all the Gaussian coefficients in case they are required. A sixth parameter can also be given to the `GaussianBlur` function, which is how borders will behave. This parameters works just like the `int borderType` parameter from the *Averaging* section.

An example of how to use `GaussianBlur` can be taken from the sample `imageFilter` project from this chapter:

```
Imgproc.GaussianBlur(image, output,  new Size(3.0, 3.0), 0);
```

The preceding line sets sigma to `0` and makes the function calculate it from the kernel's size by using the following formula:

```
sigma = 0.3*((ksize-1)*0.5 - 1) + 0.8
```

Here, `ksize` is the kernel's aperture size, which would be `3` for our example.

Median filtering

Another idea to make a filter is to select the median pixel in a kernel instead of the mean value, which is to select the pixel that would be in the middle of a line of intensity-sorted pixels. This is accomplished by using the following function:

```
public static void medianBlur(Mat src,
                              Mat dst,
                              int ksize)
```

The `Mat src` and `dst` parameters are the input and output images, respectively, while `int ksize` is the kernel's aperture size, which must be odd and greater than 1.

Sometimes, the image noise is very high and it can appear as large isolated outlier points, which would cause a noticeable average shift. In order to overcome these problems, a median filter can be used to ignore these outliers.

Bilateral filtering

While median, Gaussian, and averaging filters tend to smoothen noise and edges, the main advantage of using bilateral filtering is the fact that it will preserve them, since they present important information, such as, the boundary of a cell in some medical imaging, which should not be filtered out. The tricky part of this filter is that it considers both the spatial distance and pixel intensity difference when calculating the average, which means that it will not include pixels that have intensity differences above a given threshold when calculating the output image. Note the effect of bilateral filtering in a marble checkboard using the `imageFilter` sample project from this chapter:

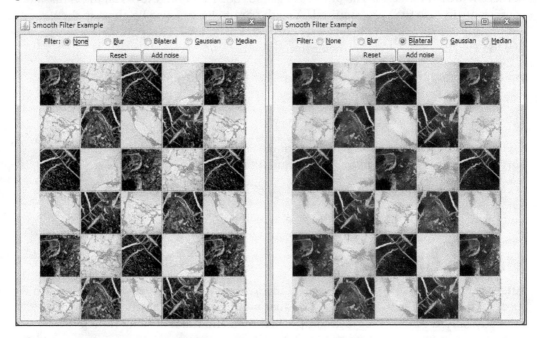

The right-hand image shows a filtered marble while preserving the edges, something that does not happen when you use other filters. One of the drawbacks of this method is that soft texture details tend to be removed, like in the white square of the third line and second column of the previous image. The function signature is as follows:

```
public static void bilateralFilter(Mat src, Mat dst, int d,
                        double sigmaColor,
                        double sigmaSpace,
                        [int borderType])
```

While `Mat src` and `Mat dst` are the input and output images, respectively, the `int d` parameter is the diameter of the considered neighborhood. If it is non-positive, the diameter will be calculated from the `sigmaSpace` parameter. The filter sigma in color space is defined by the `double sigmaColor` parameter, which means that for higher values, farther colors in the neighborhood will be considered when calculating the output color of a pixel, creating a watercolor effect. `Double sigmaSpace` is the sigma value in the coordinate space, which means that as long as colors are not skipped because of `sigmaColor`, they will have pretty much the same average component as in Gaussian. Remember that the watercolor effect can be very useful as a first step when segmenting images. If you need control over the border type, the `int borderType` parameter can be added as the last one, like in the previous filters.

When considering intensity differences to calculate the new average value of a pixel, another Gaussian function is used. Note that because of this additional step, bilateral filtering should be used with smaller kernel sizes (for instance, 5) when dealing with real-time images, while a kernel of size 9 might be good enough for offline applications. Note that when using a 3 x 3 neighborhood for a kernel of size 3, only 9 pixels are verified in the convolution of each pixel. On the other hand, when using a kernel of size 9, 9 x 9 pixels are verified, which makes the algorithm search for around 81 pixels. This could take 9 times longer.

Morphological operators

Some image operations are called morphological operations, since they change the shape of an underlying object. We will discuss erosion and dilation, which are some very useful morphological transformations in this section as well as some derived transformations. They usually appear in the context of isolating elements, removing noise, and joining distanced elements in an image.

These operators work through the convolution of a given kernel with the image. This kernel is described with an anchor point, which is the one that is probed against a region of pixels, depending on its shape:

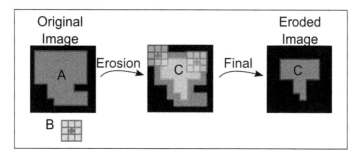

The preceding image shows a bright region on the image, which we will call **A**. Note that the complement region is completely dark. Our kernel is made of a 3 x 3 block with an anchor at its center, described as **B**. The **C** region is the result of applying the erosion morphological transformation over the image. Note that this operation takes place when you scan each pixel of the image, center the kernel anchor on each of these pixels, and then retrieve the local minimum over the kernel area. Note that erosion will reduce the bright areas.

The opposite operation is called dilation and the difference between these two is that in dilation, instead of computing the local minimum over the kernel area it will compute the local maximum over that area. This operation will expand a bright region of 3 x 3 square blocked kernels.

In order to get a better picture of how these operators work, a good idea is to try the `morphology` project from this chapter's source code. It is basically OpenCV's official C++ `morphology2` example translated to Java with some minor GUI enhancements. Note that in case of multichannel images, each channel is processed independently. The following screenshot shows the running application:

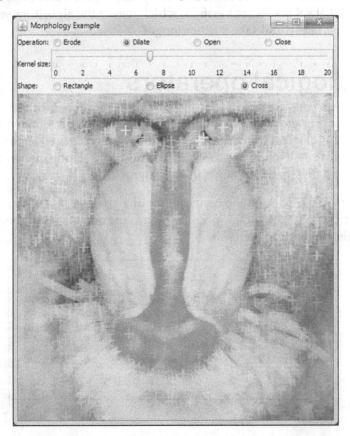

Note that our kernel bounding box is 2 times the kernel size slider parameter plus 1, so, if the kernel size parameter is selected as 1, we will have a 3 x 3 kernel bounding box. We also described our example in terms of a square kernel, but it could be of any shape, so the shape parameter is also there for us to choose from. In order to create these kernels easily, Imgproc's `getStructuringElement` function is used. This function will take the kernel's shape, its size, and zero indexed anchor position as its parameters. The kernel shape can be `Imgproc.CV_SHAPE_RECT` (for rectangles), `Imgproc.CV_SHAPE_ELLIPSE` (for ellipses), or `Imgproc.CV_SHAPE_CROSS` (for a cross-shaped kernel).

We have put all image operations in the `ImageProcessor` class, which we will highlight in the following code:

```
public Mat erode(Mat input, int elementSize, int elementShape){
  Mat outputImage = new Mat();
  Mat element = getKernelFromShape(elementSize, elementShape);
  Imgproc.erode(input,outputImage, element);
  return outputImage;
}

public Mat dilate(Mat input, int elementSize, int elementShape) {
  Mat outputImage = new Mat();
  Mat element = getKernelFromShape(elementSize, elementShape);
  Imgproc.dilate(input,outputImage, element);
  return outputImage;
}

public Mat open(Mat input, int elementSize, int elementShape) {
  Mat outputImage = new Mat();
  Mat element = getKernelFromShape(elementSize, elementShape);
  Imgproc.morphologyEx(input,outputImage, Imgproc.MORPH_OPEN,
element);
  return outputImage;
}

public Mat close(Mat input, int elementSize, int elementShape) {
  Mat outputImage = new Mat();
  Mat element = getKernelFromShape(elementSize, elementShape);
  Imgproc.morphologyEx(input,outputImage, Imgproc.MORPH_CLOSE,
element);
  return outputImage;
}

private Mat getKernelFromShape(int elementSize, int elementShape) {
   return Imgproc.getStructuringElement(elementShape, new
Size(elementSize*2+1, elementSize*2+1), new Point(elementSize,
elementSize) );
}
```

As all our methods create a kernel in the same way, we have extracted the `getKernelFromShape` method, which will simply call the `getStructuringElement` function with the size described in the preceding code. As we have a custom kernel, we will call the overloaded `Imgproc.erode` function with the input image, output image, and kernel as a third parameter. The following screenshot is a result of the erosion function over a given input image:

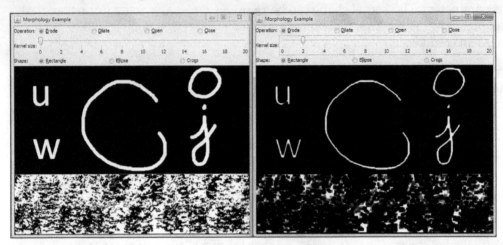

Note that this operator is frequently used to remove speckle noise from an image, as it will be eroded to nothing, while larger regions that contain important information will practically not be affected. Note that smoothing filters will not completely remove speckle noise as they tend to decrease its amplitude. Also pay attention that these operations are sensitive to kernel size, so a size adjustment and some experimenting is required. We can also check out the result of applying dilation in the following screenshot:

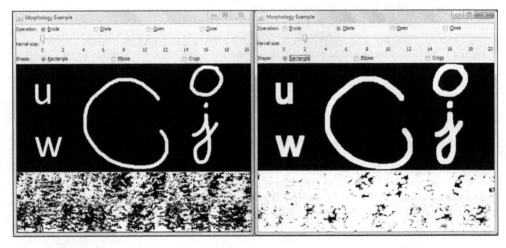

Note that besides making areas thicker, the dilate morphological transformation is also very useful in searching for connected components, which are large regions of similar pixel intensity. It might be necessary when a large region is broken into smaller ones because of shadows, noise, or other effects, as can be seen in the lower part of the image in the preceding screenshot. Applying dilation will make them link together to a bigger element.

We also derived morphological transformations, which are **open** and **close**. Open is defined by erosion followed by a dilation, while in a close operation, the dilation happens first. The following is a screenshot of an open transform:

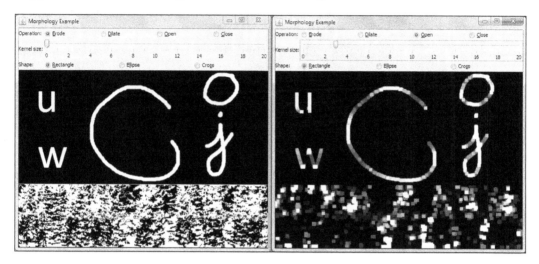

This operation is generally used while counting regions from a binary image. For example, we might use it to separate regions that are too near each other before counting them. Note that in the bottom part of our example, only larger areas have survived the operation while preserving the non-connectedness between the large areas that were apart. On the other hand, we can see the effects of applying the close operation to the same image, as shown in the following screenshot:

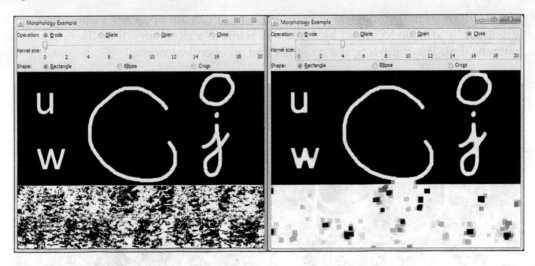

Check whether this tends to connect nearby regions. Depending on the kernel size, it might be useful in connected component algorithms to reduce segments generated by noise. Unlike erosion and dilation, both open and close morphological transformations tend to preserve the areas of their regions of interest.

Flood filling

Another very important algorithm for segmentation is flood fill, also known as region growing. Most of you who have already worked with popular computer graphic programs, such as Microsoft Paint or GIMP will have probably used the bucket fill or paint bucket tool, which fills an area with a color. Although it might look like a very simple algorithm at first sight, it has a very interesting implementation and has several parameters that can make it work well to segment images.

The idea behind the algorithm is to check for connected components, which are the areas with similar color or brightness, starting from a given point—the so-called seed point—and then examining this particular point's neighbors. These can include either 4 (north, south, east, and west) or 8 neighbors (north, north-east, east, south-east, south, south-west, west, and north-west) that check for a condition and then recursively, call the same procedure on each of the neighbors in case they have passed that condition. It will, naturally, add that point to the given connected component in case the condition is true. We generally seek for pixels that are either like the seed point or like their neighbor points, depending on which mode of flood fill will operate. We call it a fixed range when pixels are compared against the seed point and we call it a floating range when pixels are compared against neighbor pixels. This condition also accepts lower difference *loDiff* and higher difference *upDiff* parameters, which enter in the condition according to the $src(x',y') - loDiff < src(x,y) < src(x',y') + upDiff$ equation. In this equation, $src(x,y)$ is the value of the pixel at the x, y coordinates that are tested to check whether it belongs to the same domain as the seed point, while $src(x',y')$ is the value of one of the pixels that is already known to belong to that component in case of a grayscale image operating in a floating range. In case we have a fixed range flood fill, the equation turns into $src(seed.x,seed.y) - loDiff < src(x,y) < src(seed.x,seed.y) + upDiff$, where *seed.x* and *seed.y* are the seed's coordinates. Also note that in case of a colored image, each of the pixel's components are tested against the condition, while *loDiff* and *highDiff* are tridimensional scalars. All in all, a new pixel will be added to the domain in case its brightness or color is close enough to one of its neighbors that already belongs to the connected component in case of a floating range flood fill or close enough to the seed's properties in the case of a fixed range one.

The flood fill's signature is as follows:

```
public static int floodFill(Mat image,
                            Mat mask,
                            Point seedPoint,
                            Scalar newVal,
                            Rect rect,
                            Scalar loDiff,
                            Scalar upDiff,
                            int flags)
```

The `Mat image` parameter is the input/output `Mat` containing the image to perform the flood fill, while `Mat mask` is a single channel 8-bit mat 2 rows taller and 2 columns wider than `Mat image`, for performance reasons. The `Point seedpoint` parameter contains the coordinates of the seed point, while `Rect rect` is an output rectangle with the smallest bounding box that contains the segmented area. The `Scalar loDiff` and `upDiff` parameters are discussed in the preceding condition. The `int flags` parameter contains options for the operating mode of the algorithm. The source code containing a *façade* class for the `floodFill` method is available in the `floodfill` project in this chapter. The following is a screenshot of the application:

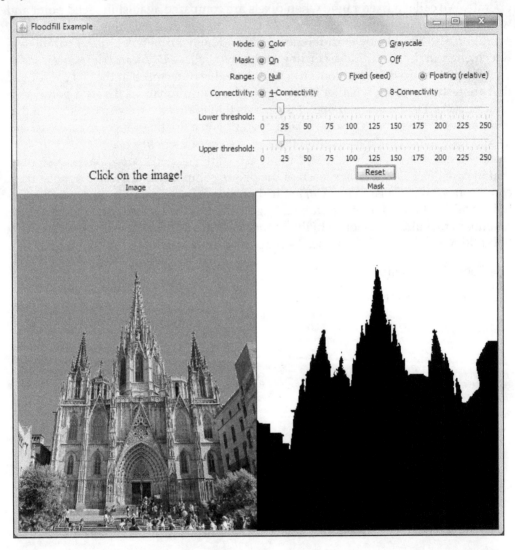

On the left-hand side of the preceding screenshot, there is a `JLabel` like the one explained in *Chapter 2, Handling Matrices, Files, Cameras, and GUIs*, used to load images, but this one has `MouseListener` that sends the captured clicks to the `FloodFillFacade` class. On the right-hand side of the preceding screenshot, the mask is shown in case the **Mask** radio button is turned on. The algorithm operation mode is chosen through the `Range` radio buttons, which will be relative (checks the conditions against neighbors), fixed (the condition is probed against the seed), or null (when `loDiff` and `hiDiff` are both zero). A radio button for connectivity is also available for 4 or 8 neighbors, while the lower and upper thresholds refer to the `loDiff` and `hiDiff` parameters, respectively.

While most fields from `FloodFillFacade` are just `getters` and `setters`, the flag configuration is something that you need to pay attention to. Note that a *façade* is just an object that creates a simplified interface to a larger part of code, making it easier to use. Here are some important pieces of `FloodFillFacade`:

```
public class FloodFillFacade {

    public static final int NULL_RANGE = 0;
    public static final int FIXED_RANGE = 1;
    public static final int FLOATING_RANGE = 2;
    private boolean colored = true;
    private boolean masked = true;
    private int range = FIXED_RANGE;
    private Random random = new Random();
    private int connectivity = 4;
    private int newMaskVal = 255;
    private int lowerDiff = 20;
    private int upperDiff = 20;

    public int fill(Mat image, Mat mask, int x, int y) {
        Point seedPoint = new Point(x,y);

        int b = random.nextInt(256);
        int g = random.nextInt(256);
        int r = random.nextInt(256);
        Rect rect = new Rect();

        Scalar newVal = isColored() ? new Scalar(b, g, r) : new
Scalar(r*0.299 + g*0.587 + b*0.114);

        Scalar lowerDifference = new Scalar(lowerDiff,lowerDiff,lowerDi
ff);
        Scalar upperDifference = new Scalar(upperDiff,upperDiff,upperDi
ff);
```

```
        if(range == NULL_RANGE){
            lowerDifference = new Scalar (0,0,0);
            upperDifference = new Scalar (0,0,0);
        }
        int flags = connectivity + (newMaskVal << 8) +
            (range == FIXED_RANGE ? Imgproc.FLOODFILL_FIXED_RANGE : 0);
        int area = 0;
        if(masked){
            area = Imgproc.floodFill(image, mask, seedPoint, newVal, rect,
    lowerDifference, upperDifference, flags);
        }
        else{
            area = Imgproc.floodFill(image, new Mat(), seedPoint, newVal,
    rect, lowerDifference, upperDifference, flags);
        }
        return area;
    }
    ...
    }
```

Here, firstly, `newVal` is created as the new color that is to be filled in the connected component. Java random classes are used to generate the color and in case it's a grayscale image, it is converted to grayscale. Then, we set the `lowerDifference` and `higherDifference` scalars, which will be used in accordance with the equations described previously. Then, the `flags` variable is defined. Note that connectivity is set on lower bits, while `newMaskVal` is shifted to the left 8 times. This parameter is the color used to fill the mask in case it's being used. Then, in case a fixed range is required for flood fill, its flag is set. We are then able to chose from the masked or unmasked version of flood fill. Pay attention to `new Mat()`, which is passed when does not use a mask. Observe that the `seedPoint` parameter is built from the given coordinates from our `MouseListener`.

Image pyramids

Image pyramids are simply a collection of images obtained by downsampling an original image, so that each image is one-fourth the area of its predecessor. It is mainly used in image segmentation, since it can generate a very meaningful representation of the image in low resolution, so that a time consuming algorithm can run on it. This makes it easy for us to map this result back to a higher resolution image in the pyramid and makes it possible to refine the results there. Besides, an approximation to a Laplacian, by means of difference of Gaussians, can be generated. Note that a Laplacian image is the one that will show its edges.

In order to produce the downsample image, which we will call the layer `i+1` in the Gaussian pyramid (`Gi+1`), we first convolve `Gi` with a Gaussian kernel, just like in Gaussian filtering, followed by removing every even numbered row and column. Then, we yield an image with one quarter of the area of the above layer. Averaging before downsampling is important because this way, information from odd numbered columns and rows gets captured. The function to get a downsampled image has the following signature:

```
public static void pyrDown(Mat src, Mat dst ,[Size dstsize, int
borderType])
```

The `Mat src` and `Mat dst` parameters are the input and output images. Note that the output image will have a width of `(src.width+1)/2` and a height of `(src.height+1)/2`, where / denotes an integer division. You should be careful when working with odd dimensions, since an upsampled image generated from a downsampled one will not have the same dimensions. Take for instance, an 11 x 11 image. When you use `pyrDown`, it will become a 6 x 6 image. In case you upsample it, it will become a 12 x 12 image, so you can't add or subtract it from the original image. Note that when using `pyrDown`, a 5 x 5 Gaussian kernel is used. In case you want, the `pyrDown` function is overloaded with the `Size dstsize` and `int borderType` properties. The `dstsize` property will allow you to define the output image size, but you must satisfy the following conditions:

```
|dstsize.width  * 2 - src.cols| < 2
|dstsize.height * 2 - src.rows| < 2
```

This means that you won't have much freedom when deciding the output image size. Also, `borderType` follows the same considerations as those are given in the *Smoothing* section.

On the other hand, the `pyrUp` function will upsample an image and then blur it. First, it will inject zero rows and columns on even locations and then, it convolve with the same kernel from the pyramid down operation. Note that `pyrDown` is a transformation that loses information, so `pyrUp` won't be able to recover the original image. Its usage is as follows:

```
public static void pyrUp(Mat src, Mat dst)
```

Also, its parameters are just like the `pyrDown` parameters.

In case you want to build the Laplacian, just note that it can be achieved by using the following equation:

$$L_i = G_i - \text{UP}(G_{i+1}) \otimes \mathcal{G}_{5\times5}$$

UP is the upsampling operation and ⊗G5 is the convolution with a 5 x 5 Gaussian kernel. Since `pyrUp` has already been implemented as an upsampling followed by a Gaussian blurring, all we need to do is downsample the original image, upsample it, and then subtract it from the original image. This can be accomplished by using the following code, as it appears in this chapter's `imagePyramid` sample:

```
Mat gp1 = new Mat();
Imgproc.pyrDown(image, gp1);
Imgproc.pyrUp(gp1, gp1);
Core.subtract(image, gp1, gp1);
```

In the preceding code, we assume that `image` is the image we are working on. Be careful when upsampling and then subtracting an image, since if the original image dimension is odd, they will have different dimensions. The `Core.subtract` function simply subtracts one image from another, as shown in the following screenshot:

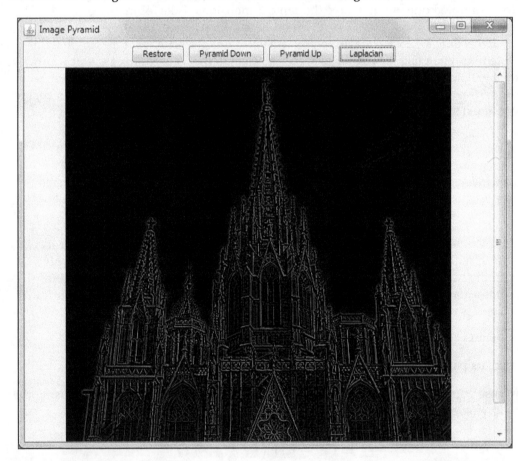

In order to see some code working with pyramids, consider checking out this chapter's imagePyramid project. The preceding screenshot shows the application running the Laplacian filter. Also, play with the buttons to get a feeling of how pyramids work.

Thresholding

One of the simplest methods of segmenting a grayscale image is using the threshold technique. It will basically set pixels below a given value as belonging to the interested object and the other pixels as not being part of it. Although it might suffer from illumination issues as well as problems that arise from variation inside the object, this can be enough when segmenting text in a page scan for OCR or to find a checkboard when calibrating the camera. Besides, some more interesting approaches, such as the adaptive threshold, can also yield good results in images that suffer from non-homogeneous lightning.

Basic thresholding is accomplished by means of Imgproc's threshold function, whose signature is as follows:

```
public static double threshold(Mat src,
                               Mat dst,
                               double thresh,
                               double maxval,
                               int type)
```

The Mats src and dst parameters are the input and output matrices, while thresh is the level used to threshold the image. double maxval is only used in the Binary and Binary_Inv modes and this will be explained in the following table. The type are Imgproc's constants used to describe the thresholding type, as in the following table, when tested in the next condition, the source pixel value is greater than the given threshold:

Thresholding type	Output when true	Output when false
CV_THRESH_BINARY	maxval	0
CV_THRESH_BINARY_INV	0	maxval
CV_THRESH_BINARY	threshold	source value
CV_TOZERO	source value	0
CV_TOZERO_INV	0	source value

The following diagram will help you to easily understand the preceding table:

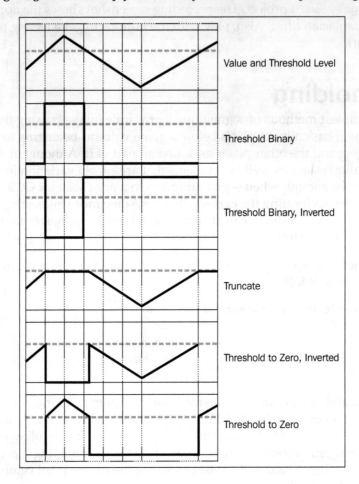

When thresholding, it is important to experiment with several values using, for instance, a slider bar. The sample project `threshold` from this chapter makes it really easy to change the function's arguments and test the results. A screenshot of the project is shown as follows:

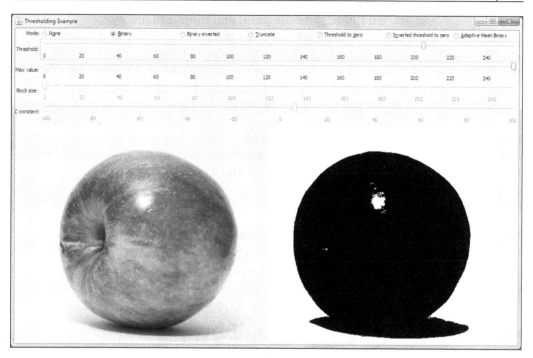

Note that although the apple might pose a simple problem for segmentation, when applying the binary thresholding method, the apple is almost completely identified, except for the lighting spot above the middle line, which clearly has pixels above the 205 level, since they are almost pure white, which would be the 255 level. Besides, the shadow area under the apple is also identified as belonging to it. Aside from these minor problems, it is simple to use and will generally be part of one of the steps in any computer vision application.

Another interesting approach to this type of segmentation is related to the use of a dynamic threshold value. Instead of using a given value, the threshold is calculated as a mean of a square block around each pixel minus a given constant. This method is implemented in OpenCV through the `adaptiveThreshold` function, which has the following signature:

```
public static void adaptiveThreshold(Mat src,
                                     Mat dst,
                                     double maxValue,
                                     int adaptiveMethod,
                                     int thresholdType,
                                     int blockSize,
                                     double C)
```

The `Mat src` and `dst` parameters are the input and output matrices, respectively. `Maxvalue` is used the same way as the ordinary threshold function, which is described in the preceding section. The adaptive method can either be `ADAPTIVE_THRESH_MEAN_C` or `ADAPTIVE_THRESH_GAUSSIAN_C`. The first one will calculate the mean as the pixel value sum divided by the number of pixels in the block, while the latter will use Gaussian weighting for the average. `BlockSize` is the square `blockSize` by the `blockSize` region used for the mean whose value must be odd and greater than 1. The `C` constant is the value subtracted from the mean to compose the dynamic threshold. Note the result obtained for the same image with the adaptive threshold using `blocksize` of `13` and a constant `C` of `6`:

Note that the shadow area is now much better, although the irregular texture from the apple can cause other problems. The sample code uses a binary and `ADAPTIVE_THRESH_MEAN_C` adaptive thresholding, but changing it for Gaussian is just a matter of changing the type parameter.

Summary

This chapter explained the theory and practice of basic image processing operations that will be required in any computer vision project. We started with filters that work with simple average or using a Gaussian weighting as well as a median and discussed the interesting bilateral filter, which maintains edges. Then, we explored the important morphological operators, such as erosion, dilation, opening, and closing, which appear in the context of isolating elements, removing noise, and joining distanced elements in an image. We followed this with the well-known paint bucket operation through flood filling. Then, we explored time and processing saving image pyramids, which make segmentation faster in higher levels by decreasing the image area to one quarter in each layer. We finally explained the important image segmentation technique called thresholding and tested the adaptive thresholding as well.

In the next chapter, we will focus on important image transforms, which will allow us to find edges, lines, and circles in images. Then, you will learn stretch, shrink, warp, and rotate operations, which will be followed by the Fourier transform, which is a nice tool to change image from the spatial domain to the frequency domain. Finally, we will check out integral images, which boost some face-tracking algorithms.

4
Image Transforms

This chapter covers the methods to change an image into an alternate representation of data in order to cover important problems of computer vision and image processing. Some examples of these methods are artifacts that are used to find image edges as well as transforms that help us find lines and circles in an image. In this chapter, we have covered stretch, shrink, warp, and rotate operations. A very useful and famous transform is Fourier, which transforms signals between the time domain and frequency domain. In OpenCV, you can find the **Discrete Fourier Transform (DFT)** and **Discrete Cosine Transform (DCT)**. Another transform that we've covered in this chapter is related to integral images that allow rapid summing of sub regions, which is a very useful step in tracking faces algorithm. Besides this, you will also get to see distance transform and histogram equalization in this chapter.

we will cover the following topics:

- Gradients and sobel derivatives
- The Laplace and canny transforms
- The line and circle Hough transforms
- Geometric transforms: stretch, shrink, warp, and rotate
- Discrete Fourier Transform (DFT) and Discrete Cosine Transform (DCT)
- Integral images
- Distance transforms
- Histogram equalization

By the end of this chapter, you will have learned a handful of transforms that will enable you to find edges, lines, and circles in images. Besides, you will be able to stretch, shrink, warp, and rotate images as well as you will be able to change the domain from the spatial domain to the frequency domain. Other important transforms used for face tracking will be covered in this chapter as well. Finally, distance transforms and histogram equalization will also be explored in detail.

The Gradient and Sobel derivatives

A key building block in computer vision is finding edges and this is closely related to finding an approximation to derivatives in an image. From basic calculus, it is known that a derivative shows the variation of a given function or an input signal with some dimension. When we find the local maximum of the derivative, this will yield regions where the signal varies the most, which for an image might mean an edge. Hopefully, there's an easy way to approximate a derivative for discrete signals through a kernel convolution. A convolution basically means applying some transforms to every part of the image. The most used transform for differentiation is the Sobel filter [1], which works for horizontal, vertical, and even mixed partial derivatives of any order.

In order to approximate the value for the horizontal derivative, the following sobel kernel matrix is convoluted with an input image:

$$G_x = \begin{bmatrix} -1 & 0 & +1 \\ -2 & 0 & 2 \\ -1 & 0 & 1 \end{bmatrix} * T_x$$

This means that, for each input pixel, the calculated value of its upper-right neighbor plus twice its right neighbor, plus its bottom-right neighbor, minus its upper-left neighbor, minus its left neighbor, minus its left-bottom neighbor will be calculated, yielding a resulting image. In order to use this operator in OpenCV, you can call Imgproc's `Sobel` function according to the following signature:

```
public static void Sobel(Mat src, Mat dst, int ddepth, int dx, int dy)
```

The `src` parameter is the input image and `dst` is the output. `Ddepth` is the output image's depth and when this is assigned as `-1`, this has the same depth as the source. The `dx` and `dy` parameters will inform us about the order in each of these directions. When setting `dy` to `0` and `dx` to `1`, the kernel that we've used is the one mentioned in the preceding matrix. The example project `kernels` from this chapter shows a customizable look of these operators, as shown in the following screenshot:

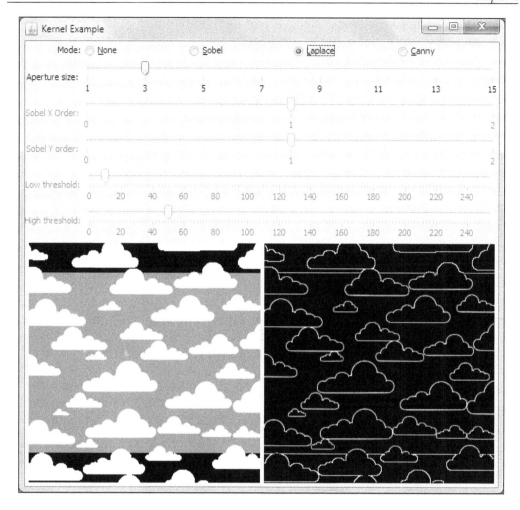

The Laplace and Canny transforms

Another quite useful operator to find edges is the Laplacian transformation. Instead of relying on the first order derivatives, OpenCV's Laplacian transformation implements the discrete operator for the following function:

$$Laplace(f) = \frac{\partial^2 f}{\partial x^2} + \frac{\partial^2 f}{\partial y^2}$$

The matrix can be approximated to the convolution with the following kernel when using finite difference methods and a 3x3 aperture:

$$\begin{bmatrix} 0 & 1 & 0 \\ 1 & -4 & 1 \\ 0 & 1 & 0 \end{bmatrix}$$

The signature for the preceding function is as follows:

```
Laplacian(Mat source, Mat destination, int ddepth)
```

While source and destination matrices are simple parameters, `ddepth` is the depth of the destination matrix. When you set this parameter to `-1`, it will have the same depth as the source image, although you might want more depth when you apply this operator. Besides this, there are overloaded versions of this method that receive an aperture size, a scale factor, and an adding scalar.

Besides using the Laplacian method, you can also use the Canny algorithm, which is an excellent approach that was proposed by computer scientist John F. Canny, who optimized edge detection for low error rate, single identification, and correct localization. In order to fulfill it, the Canny algorithm applies a Gaussian to filter the noise, calculates intensity gradients through sobel, suppresses spurious responses, and applies double thresholds followed by a hysteresis that suppresses the weak and unconnected edges. For more information, check this paper [2]. The method's signature is as follows:

```
Canny(Mat image, Mat edges, double threshold1, double threshold2, int
apertureSize, boolean L2gradient)
```

The `image` parameter is the input matrix, `edges` is the output image, `threshold1` is the first threshold for the hysteresis procedure (values smaller than this will be ignored), and `threshold2` is the high threshold for hysteresis (values higher than this will be considered as strong edges, while the smaller values and the ones higher than the low threshold will be checked for connection with strong edges). The aperture size is used for the Sobel operator when calculating the gradient and the `boolean` informs us which norm to use for the gradient. You can also check out the source code to use this operator in the kernel's project sample in this chapter.

The line and circle Hough transforms

In case you need to find straight lines or circles in an image, you can use Hough transforms, as they are very useful. In this section, we will cover OpenCV methods to extract them from your image.

The idea behind the original Hough line transform is that any point in a binary image could be part of a set of lines. Suppose each straight line could be parameterized by the $y = mx + b$ line equation, where m is the line slope and b is the y axis intercept of this line. Now, we could iterate the whole binary image, storing each of the m and b parameters and checking their accumulation. The local maximum points of the m and b parameters would yield equations of straight lines that mostly appeared in the image. Actually, instead of using the slope and y axis interception point, we use the polar straight line representation.

Since OpenCV not only supports the standard Hough transform, but also the progressive probabilistic Hough transform for which the two functions are `Imgproc.HoughLines` and `Imgproc.HoughLinesP`, respectively. For detailed information, refer to [3]. These functions' signatures are explained as follows:

```
HoughLines(Mat image, Mat lines, double rho, double theta, int
threshold)
HoughLinesP(Mat image, Mat lines, double rho, double theta, int
threshold)
```

The `hough` project from this chapter shows an example of the usage of them. The following is the code to retrieve lines from `Imgproc.HoughLines`:

```
Mat canny = new Mat();
Imgproc.Canny(originalImage, canny, 10, 50, aperture, false);
image = originalImage.clone();
Mat lines = new Mat();
Imgproc.HoughLines(canny, lines, 1, Math.PI/180, lowThreshold);
```

Note that we need to apply the Hough transform over an edge image; therefore, the first two lines of the preceding code will take care of this. Then, the original image is cloned for display and a `Mat` object is created in the fourth line in order to keep the lines. In the last line, we can see the application of `HoughLines`.

The third parameter in `Imgproc.HoughLines` refers to the distance resolution of the accumulator in pixels, while the fourth parameter is the angle resolution of the accumulator in radians. The fifth parameter is the accumulator threshold, which means that only the lines with more than the specified amount of votes will be returned. The `lowThreshold` variable is tied to the scale slider in the example application for the user to experiment with it. It is important to observe that the lines are returned in the `lines` matrix, which has two columns in which each line returns the `rho` and `theta` parameters of the polar coordinates. These coordinates refer to the distance between the top-left corner of the image and the line rotation in radians, respectively. Following this example, you will find out how to draw the lines from the returned matrix. You can see the working of the Hough transform in the following screenshot:

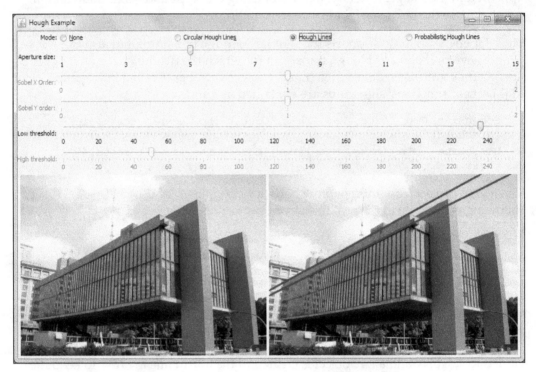

Besides having the standard Hough transform, OpenCV also offers a probabilistic Hough line transform as well as a circular version. Both the implementations are explored in the same Hough sample project, and the following screenshot shows the working of the circular version:

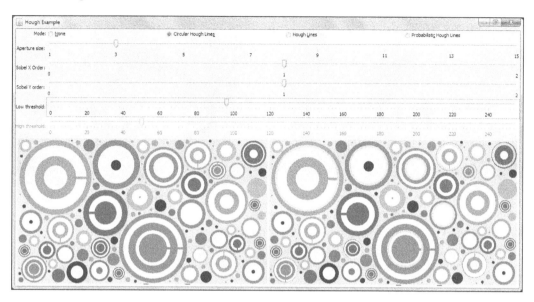

Geometric transforms – stretch, shrink, warp, and rotate

While working with images and computer vision, it is very common that you will require the ability to preprocess an image using known geometric transforms, such as stretching, shrinking, rotation, and warping. The latter is the same as nonuniform resizing. These transforms can be realized through the multiplication of source points with a 2 x 3 matrix and they get the name of **affine transformations** while turning rectangles in parallelograms. Hence, they have the limitation of requiring the destination to have parallel sides. On the other hand, a 3 x 3 matrix multiplication represents perspective transforms. They offer more flexibility since they can map a 2D quadrilateral to another. The following screenshot shows a very useful application of this concept.

Here, we will find out which is the perspective transform that maps the side of a building in a perspective view to its frontal view:

Note that the input to this problem is the perspective photograph of the building, which is seen on the left-hand side of the preceding image, as well as the four corner points of the highlighted quadrilateral shape. The output is to the right and shows what a viewer would see if he/she looks at the side of the building.

Since affine transforms are a subset of perspective transformations, we will focus on the latter ones here. The code available for this example is in the `warps` project of this chapter. The main method used here is `warpPerspective` from `Imgproc`. It applies a perspective transformation to an input image. Here is the method signature for the `warpPerspective` method:

```
public static void warpPerspective(Mat src, Mat dst, Mat M, Size
dsize)
```

The `Mat src` parameter is, naturally, the input image, which is the left-hand side image in the preceding screenshot, while `dst Mat` is the image on the right-hand side; make sure you initialize this parameter before using the method. The not-so-straightforward parameter here is `Mat M`, which is the warping matrix. In order to calculate it, you can use the `getPerspectiveTransform` method from `Imgproc` as well. This method will calculate the perspective matrix from two sets of the four correlated 2D points, the source and destination points. In our example, the source points are the ones that are highlighted on the left-hand side of the screenshot, while the destination points are the four corner points of the image to the right. These points can be stored through the `MatOfPoint2f` class, which stores the `Point` objects. The `getPerspectiveTransform` method's signature is as follows:

```
public static Mat getPerspectiveTransform(Mat src, Mat dst)
```

`Mat src` and `Mat dst` are the same as the `MatOfPoint2f` class mentioned previously, which is a subclass of `Mat`.

In our example, we added a mouse listener to retrieve points clicked by the user. A detail to be kept in mind is that these points are stored in the order: top-left, top-right, bottom-left, and bottom-right. In the example application, the currently modified point can be chosen through four radio buttons above the images. The act of clicking and dragging listeners has been added to the code, so both approaches work.

Discrete Fourier Transform and Discrete Cosine Transform

When dealing with image analysis, it would be very useful if you could change an image from the spatial domain, which is the image in terms of its x and y coordinates, to the frequency domain—the image decomposed in its high and low frequency components—so that you would be able to see and manipulate frequency parameters. This could come in handy in image compression because it is known that human vision is not much sensitive to high frequency signals as it is to low frequency signals. In this way, you could transform an image from the spatial domain to the frequency domain and remove high frequency components, reducing the required memory to represent the image and hence compressing it. An image frequency can be pictured in a better way by the next image.

In order to change an image from the spatial domain to the frequency domain, the Discrete Fourier Transform can be used. As we might need to bring it back from the frequency domain to the spatial domain, another transform, which is the Inverse Discrete Fourier Transform, can be applied.

The formal definition of DFT is as follows:

$$F(k,l) = \sum_{i=0}^{N-1} \sum_{i=0}^{N-1} f(i,j) e^{-i2\pi\left(\frac{ki}{N}+\frac{lj}{N}\right)}$$

The `f(i,j)` value is the image in the spatial domain and `F(k,l)` is the image in the frequency domain. Note that `F(k,l)` is a complex function, which means that it has a real and an imaginary part. This way, it will be represented by two OpenCV `Mat` objects or by `Mat` with two channels. The easiest way to analyze a DFT is by plotting its magnitude and taking its logarithm, since values for the DFT can be in different orders of magnitude.

For instance, this is a pulse pattern, which is a signal that can come from zero, represented as black, to the top, represented as white, on its left, and its Fourier transform magnitude with the applied logarithm to its right:

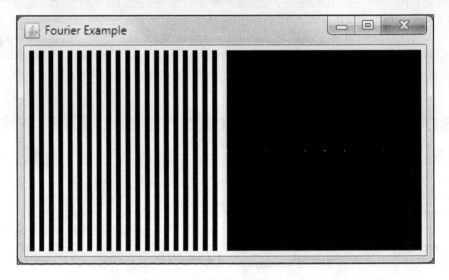

Looking back at the preceding DFT transform, we can think of F(k,l) as the value that would be yielded by multiplying each point of the spatial image with a base function, which is related to the frequency domain, and by summing the products. Remember that base functions are sinusoidal and they have increasing frequencies. This way, if some of the base functions oscillate at the same rate as the signal, it will be able to sum up to a big number, which will be seen as a white dot on the Fourier Transform image. On the other hand, if the given frequency is not present in the image, the oscillation and multiplication with the image will result in a small number, which won't be noticed in the Fourier Transform image.

Another thing to observe from the equation is that F(0,0) will yield a base function that is always 1. This way, F(0,0) will simply refer to the sum of all the pixels of the spatial image. We can also check whether F(N-1, N-1) corresponds to the base function related to the highest frequency in the image. Note that the previous image basically has a DC component, which would be the image mean and it could be checked from the white dot in the middle of the Discrete Fourier transform image. Besides, the image to the left could be seen as a series of pulses and hence it would have a frequency in the *x* axis, which can be noticed by the two dots near the central point in the Fourier Transform image to the right. Nonetheless, we will need to use multiple frequencies to approximate the pulse shape. In this way, more dots can be seen in the *x*-axis of the image to the right. The following screenshot gives more insight and helps you understand the Fourier analysis:

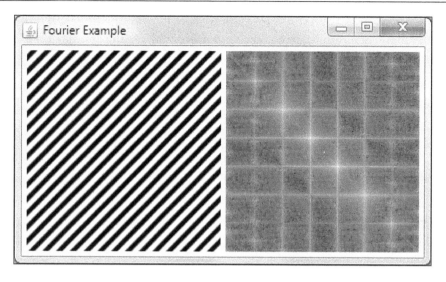

Now, we will again check the DC level at the center of the DFT image, to the right, as a bright central dot. Besides, we can also check multiple frequencies in a diagonal pattern. An important piece of information that can be retrieved is the direction of spatial variation, which is clearly seen as bright dots in the DFT image.

It is time to work on some code now. The following code shows you how to make room to apply the DFT. Remember, from the preceding screenshot, that the result of a DFT is complex. Besides, we need them stored as floating point values. This way, we first convert our 3-channel image to gray and then to a float. After this, we put the converted image and an empty `Mat` object into a list of mats, combining them into a single `Mat` object through the use of the `Core.merge` function, shown as follows:

```
Mat gray = new Mat();
Imgproc.cvtColor(originalImage, gray, Imgproc.COLOR_RGB2GRAY);
Mat floatGray = new Mat();
gray.convertTo(floatGray, CvType.CV_32FC1);

List<Mat> matList = new ArrayList<Mat>();
matList.add(floatGray);
Mat zeroMat = Mat.zeros(floatGray.size(), CvType.CV_32F);
matList.add(zeroMat);
Mat complexImage = new Mat();
Core.merge(matList, complexImage);
```

Now, it's easy to apply an in-place Discrete Fourier Transform:

```
Core.dft(complexImage,complexImage);
```

In order to get some meaningful information, we will print the image, but first, we have to obtain its magnitude. In order to get it, we will use the standard way that we learned in school, which is getting the square root of the sum of the squares of the real and complex parts of numbers.

Again, OpenCV has a function for this, which is `Core.magnitude`, whose signature is `magnitude(Mat x, Mat y, Mat magnitude)`, as shown in the following code:

```
List<Mat> splitted = new ArrayList<Mat>();
Core.split(complexImage,splitted);
Mat magnitude = new Mat();
Core.magnitude(splitted.get(0), splitted.get(1), magnitude);
```

Before using `Core.magnitude`, just pay attention to the process of unpacking a DFT in the splitted mats using `Core.split`.

Since the values can be in different orders of magnitude, it is important to get the values in a logarithmic scale. Before doing this, it is important to add `1` to all the values in the matrix just to make sure we won't get negative values when applying the `log` function. Besides this, there's already an OpenCV function to deal with logarithms, which is `Core.log`:

```
Core.add(Mat.ones(magnitude.size(), CvType.CV_32F), magnitude,
magnitude);
Core.log(magnitude, magnitude);
```

Now, it is time to shift the image to the center, so that it's easier to analyze its spectrum. The code to do this is simple and goes like this:

```
int cx = magnitude.cols()/2;
int cy = magnitude.rows()/2;
Mat q0 = new Mat(magnitude,new Rect(0, 0, cx, cy));
Mat q1 = new Mat(magnitude,new Rect(cx, 0, cx, cy));
Mat q2 = new Mat(magnitude,new Rect(0, cy, cx, cy));
Mat q3 = new Mat(magnitude ,new Rect(cx, cy, cx, cy));
Mat tmp = new Mat();
q0.copyTo(tmp);
q3.copyTo(q0);
tmp.copyTo(q3);

q1.copyTo(tmp);
q2.copyTo(q1);
tmp.copyTo(q2);
```

As a last step, it's important to normalize the image, so that it can be seen in a better way. Before we normalize it, it should be converted to CV_8UC1:

```
magnitude.convertTo(magnitude, CvType.CV_8UC1);
Core.normalize(magnitude, magnitude,0,255, Core.NORM_MINMAX, CvType.
CV_8UC1);
```

When using the DFT, it's often enough to calculate only half of the DFT when you deal with real-valued data, as is the case with images. This way, an analog concept called the Discrete Cosine Transform can be used. In case you want it, it can be invoked through `Core.dct`.

Integral images

Some face recognition algorithms, such as OpenCV's face detection algorithm make heavy use of features like the ones shown in the following image:

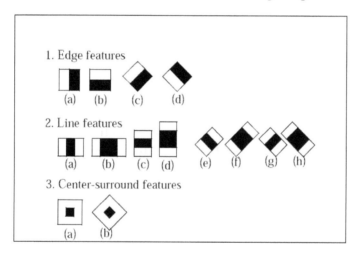

These are the so-called Haar-like features and they are calculated as the sum of pixels in the white area minus the sum of pixels in the black area. You might find this type of a feature kind of odd, but when training it for face detection, it can be built to be an extremely powerful classifier using only two of these features, as depicted in the following image:

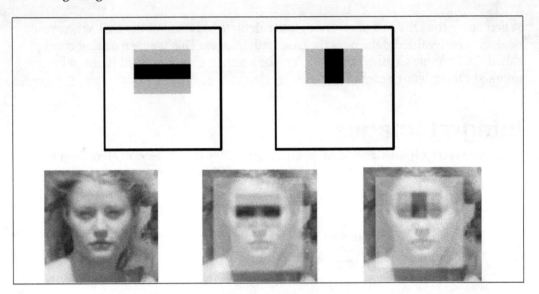

In fact, a classifier that uses only the two preceding features can be adjusted to detect 100 percent of a given face training database with only 40 percent of false positives. Taking out the sum of all pixels in an image as well as calculating the sum of each area can be a long process. However, this process must be tested for each frame in a given input image, hence calculating these features fast is a requirement that we need to fulfill.

First, let's define an integral image sum as the following expression:

$$\text{sum}(X, Y) = \sum_{x<X} \sum_{y<Y} image(x, y)$$

For instance, if the following matrix represents our image:

$$A = \begin{bmatrix} 0 & 2 & 4 \\ 6 & 8 & 10 \\ 12 & 14 & 16 \end{bmatrix}$$

An integral image would be like the following:

$$\text{Sum A}=\begin{bmatrix} 0 & 0 & 0 & 0 \\ 0 & 0 & 2 & 6 \\ 0 & 6 & 16 & 30 \\ 0 & 18 & 42 & 72 \end{bmatrix}$$

The trick here follows from the following property:

$$\sum_{x1\leq x\leq x2}\sum_{y1\leq y\leq y2} image(x,y)=sum(x2,y2)-sum(x1-1,y2)-sum(x2,y1-1)+sum(x1-1,y1-1)$$

This means that in order to find the sum of a given rectangle bounded by the points `(x1,y1)`, `(x2,y1)`, `(x2,y2)`, and `(x1,y2)`, you just need to use the integral image at the point `(x2,y2)`, but you also need to subtract the points `(x1-1,y2)` from `(x2,y1-1)`. Also, since the integral image at `(x1-1, y1-1)` has been subtracted twice, we just need to add it once.

The following code will generate the preceding matrix and make use of `Imgproc.integral` to create the integral images:

```
Mat image = new Mat(3,3 ,CvType.CV_8UC1);
Mat sum = new Mat();
byte[] buffer = {0,2,4,6,8,10,12,14,16};
image.put(0,0,buffer);
System.out.println(image.dump());
Imgproc.integral(image, sum);
System.out.println(sum.dump());
```

The output of this program is like the one shown in the preceding matrices for A and Sum A.

It is important to verify that the output is a 4 x 4 matrix because of the initial row and column of zeroes, which are used to make the computation efficient.

Distance transforms

Simply put, a distance transform applied to an image will generate an output image whose pixel values will be the closest distance to a zero-valued pixel in the input image. Basically, they will have the closest distance to the background, given a specified distance measure. The following screenshot gives you an idea of what happens to the silhouette of a human body:

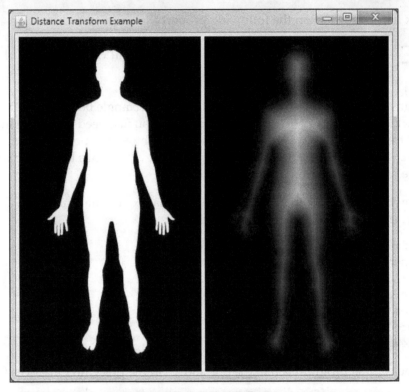

Human silhouette by J E Theriot

This transform can be very useful in the process of getting the topological skeleton of a given segmented image as well as to produce blurring effects. Another interesting application of this transform is in the segmentation of overlapping objects, along with a watershed.

Generally, the distance transform is applied to an edge image, which results from a Canny filter. We are going to make use of Imgproc's `distanceTransform` method, which can be seen in action in the `distance` project, which you can find in this chapter's source code. Here are the most important lines of this example program:

```
protected void processOperation() {
    Imgproc.Canny(originalImage, image, 220, 255, 3, false);
```

```
Imgproc.threshold(image, image, 100, 255,
    Imgproc.THRESH_BINARY_INV );
Imgproc.distanceTransform(image, image, Imgproc.CV_DIST_L2, 3);
image.convertTo(image, CvType.CV_8UC1);
Core.multiply(image, new Scalar(20), image);

updateView();
}
```

Firstly, a Canny edge detector filter is applied to the input image. Then, a threshold with `THRESH_BINARY_INV` converts the edges to black and beans to white. Only then, the distance transform is applied. The first argument is the input image, the second one is the output matrix, and the third argument specifies how distances are calculated. In our example, `CVDIST_L2` means Euclidean, while other distances, such as `CVDIST_L1` or `CVDIST_L12`, among others exist. Since the output of `distanceTtransform` is a single channel 32 bit Float image, a conversion is required. Finally, we apply `Core.multiply` to increase the contrast.

The following screenshot gives you a good idea of the whole process:

Histogram equalization

The human visual system is very sensitive to contrast in images, which is the difference in the color and brightness of different objects. Besides, the human eye is a miraculous system that can feel intensities at the 10_{16} light levels [4]. No wonder some sensors could mess up the image data.

When analyzing images, it is very useful to draw their histograms. They simply show you the lightness distribution of a digital image. In order to do that, you need to count the number of pixels with the exact lightness and plot that as a distribution graph. This gives us a great insight into the dynamic range of an image.

When a camera picture has been captured with a very narrow light range, it gets difficult to see the details in the shadowed areas or other areas with poor local contrast. Fortunately, there's a technique to spread frequencies for uniform intensity distribution, which is called **histogram equalization**. The following image shows the same picture with their respective histograms before and after the histogram equalization technique is applied:

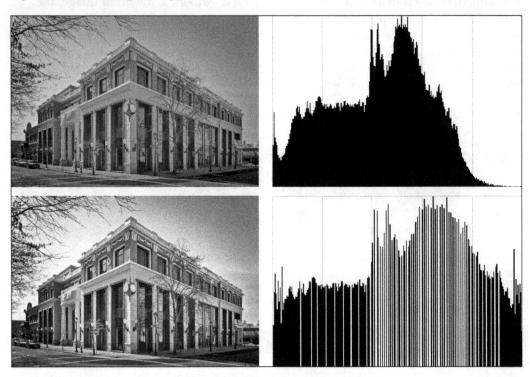

Note that the light values, located at the rightmost part of the upper histogram, are rarely used, while the middle range values are too tied. Spreading the values along the full range yields better contrast and details can be more easily perceived by this. The histogram equalized image makes better use of intensities that generate better contrast. In order to accomplish this task, a cumulative distribution can be used to remap the histogram to something that resembles a uniform distribution. Then, it's just a matter of checking where the points from the original histogram would be mapped to the uniform distribution through the use of a cumulative Gaussian distribution, for instance.

Now, the good part is that all these details have been wrapped in a simple call to OpenCV's `equalizeHist` function. Here is the sample from the `histogram` project in this chapter:

```
protected void processOperation() {
    Imgproc.cvtColor(originalImage, grayImage, Imgproc.COLOR_RGB2GRAY);
    Imgproc.equalizeHist(grayImage, image);
    updateView();
}
```

This piece of code simply converts the image to a single channel image; however, you can use `equalizeHist` on a color image as long as you treat each channel separately. The `Imgproc.equalizeHist` method outputs the corrected image following the previously mentioned concept.

References

1. *A 3x3 Isotropic Gradient Operator for Image Processing* presented at a talk at the Stanford Artificial Project in 1968, by I. Sobel and G. Feldman.

2. *A Computational Approach To Edge Detection*, IEEE Trans. Pattern Analysis and Machine Intelligence, by Canny, J.

3. *Robust Detection of Lines Using the Progressive Probabilistic Hough Transform*, CVIU 78 1, by Matas, J. and Galambos, C., and Kittler, J.V. pp 119-137 (2000).

4. *Advanced High Dynamic Range Imaging: Theory and Practice*, CRC Press, by Banterle, Francesco; Artusi, Alessandro; Debattista, Kurt; Chalmers, Alan.

Summary

This chapter covered the key aspects of computer vision's daily use. We started with the important edge detectors, where you gained the experience of how to find them through the Sobel, Laplacian, and Canny edge detectors. Then, we saw how to use the Hough transforms to find straight lines and circles. After that, the geometric transforms stretch, shrink, warp, and rotate were explored with an interactive sample. We then explored how to transform images from the spatial domain to the frequency domain using the Discrete Fourier analysis. After that, we showed you a trick to calculate Haar-like features fast in an image through the use of integral images. We then explored the important distance transforms and finished the chapter by explaining histogram equalization to you.

Now, be ready to dive into machine learning algorithms, as we will cover how to detect faces in the next chapter. Also, you will learn how to create your own object detector and understand how supervised learning works in order to better train your classification trees.

Object Detection Using Ada Boost and Haar Cascades

5

This chapter shows a very interesting feature of OpenCV — detecting faces in an image or a video stream. In the latter case, we call it **face tracking**. In order to do so, this chapter dives into machine-learning algorithms, specifically supervised learning with boosting. We will cover the **Viola-Jones classifier** and its theory as well as the details on how to use the face-trained classifiers that are bundled with OpenCV.

In this chapter, we will be covering the following topics:

- The boosting theory
- Viola-Jones classifier
- Detecting faces
- Learning new objects

By the end of this chapter, you will be able to understand the theory behind face classifiers through boosting, and the Viola-Jones classifier. You will also know how to use straightforward face classifiers. Besides, you will be able to create your own object classifier for different objects.

The boosting theory

The problem of detecting a face in an image can be posed in a simpler way. We could iterate the whole image through several smaller windows and create a classifier that will tell whether a window is a face or not. The windows that correctly identify the face will be the coordinates of face detection.

Now, what exactly is a classifier and how can it be built? In machine learning, the problem of classification has been deeply explored and it is posed as the identification of which of the set of categories a given observation belongs to, based on a previously trained set of known category memberships. This could be something like if a given image belongs to the banana, apple, or grape category, for instance, in a fruit classification application. In the case of face detection, there are two categories—face and non-face.

This section describes a meta-algorithm, which is basically a templated algorithm to create a strong classifier using a set of weak learners. These weak learners are classifiers based on some features that although not able to divide the whole set in the two categories, they do a good job for some of the sets. Let's say that a weak learner could be a classifier that looks for a mustache in order to tell whether a given face is of a man. Even if it might not find all men in the set, it will do a good job for the ones who have mustaches.

AdaBoost

AdaBoosting, from Adaptive Boosting, is not actually an algorithm, but it's a meta-algorithm that will help us with building a classifier. Its main mission is to build a great classifier out of weak classifiers, which are just better by chance. Its final form is a weighted combination of the given classifiers, as given in the following equation:

$$H(x) = sign\big(\alpha_1 h_1(x) + \alpha_2 h_2(x) + \ldots + \alpha_T h_T(x)\big)$$

The sign operator will return +1 when the expression in parenthesis is positive, and -1 otherwise. Note that it is a binary classifier that yields *yes* or *no*, or it could be *does belong* or *does not belong*, or simply +1 or -1. So, α_t is the weight assigned to the given classifier $h_t(x)$ for a given input x in a set of T classifiers.

For instance, in a group of people, one wants to know whether any given person p is a man or woman. Let's say we have some weak classifiers, which are good guesses, such as:

- h_1: If the height is greater than 5 feet and 9 inches (~175 cm), then the person is a male or else female. Of course, there are several women taller than men, but on an average, men are taller.

- h_2: If a person has long hair, then the person is a female or else male. Again, there are several long haired men, but, on an average, women usually have longer hair.

- h_3: If a person has a beard, then the person is a male or else female. Here, we can misclassify shaved men.

Let's say we have this random set of people:

Name/Feature	Height (h1)	Hair (h2)	Beard (h3)	Gender (f(x))
Katherine	1.69	Long	Absent	Female
Dan	1.76	Short	Absent	Male
Sam	1.80	Short	Absent	Male
Laurent	1.83	Short	Present	Male
Sara	1.77	Short	Absent	Female

Classifier h1 will correctly classify three people, while h2 will get it right for four people, and h3 will work for three people. We would then select h2, which was the best, for the one that minimizes the weighted error, and set its alpha. We would then increase weight for wrongly classified data (Sara) and decrease weight for all the others (Katherine, Dan, Sam, and Laurent). We would then look for the best classifier on the new distribution. Now that Sara is on the spot, either h2 or h3 would be selected, depending on the error, since h1 gets Sara wrong with a higher weight. We would then continue for the T weak classifiers, in our case 3.

The algorithm for AdaBoost goes like this:

1. $D_1(i) = 1/m, i = 1,...,m$.

2. For $t = 1,...,T$:

   a. Find the classifier h_t that minimizes the $D_t(i)$ weighted error:

   b. $h_t = \arg\min_{h_j \in H} \varepsilon_j$, where $\varepsilon_j = \sum_{i=1}^{m} D_t(i)$ (for $y_i \neq h_j(x_i)$) as long as $\varepsilon_j < 0.5$; else quit.

   c. Set the h_t voting weight $\alpha_t = \frac{1}{2}\log[(1-\varepsilon_t)/\varepsilon_t]$, where ε_t is the arg min error from step 2b.

   d. Update the data point weights: $D_{t+1}(i) = [D_t(i)\exp(-\alpha_t y_i h_t(x_i))]/Z_t$, where Z_t normalizes the equation over all data points i.

Fortunately, OpenCV already implements boosting. The following example can be found in the `boost` project from `Chapter 5`, and it shows how to deal with the `Boost` class, with the preceding example. We first create a 5 x 3 matrix called `data`. This matrix stores our training dataset, and will be used by `Boost` to create a classifier. Then, we feed the matrix just like in the preceding table. The first column is the height. Hair and beard are given values one or zero. When the hair is short, we put `zero`, when it's long, we put `one`. In case the beard is present, its value is `one` or else `zero`. These values are set using the Mat's `put` function. Note that the fact of being a man or a woman does not go into the `data` matrix since it is actually the output we want for our classifier. This way, a 5 x 1 column matrix `responses` is created. It simply stores `zero` for female and `one` for male.

Then, a `Boost` class is instantiated, and we set parameters for the training through the `CvBoostParams` its setters. We have set the boost type to be **Discrete Adaboost** using the `setBoostType` method, passing `Boost.DISCRETE` as a parameter. Other variants of boosting are known as **Real AdaBoost**, **LogitBoost**, and **Gentle AdaBoost**. The setWeakCount method sets the number of weak classifiers used. In our case, it was 3. The next setting tells that if the number of samples in a node is less than this parameter, then the node will not be split. Actually, the default value is 10, and it won't work with such a small dataset, so it is set to 4 so that it will work with this dataset. It is important to note that Boost derives from DTrees, which is decision-trees related. That's why, it uses the node terminology.

After parameters are set, the boost classifier is trained using the `data` and `responses` matrices through the `train` method. Here follows this method signature:

```
public boolean train(Mat trainData, int tflag, Mat responses)
```

This is the `trainData` training matrix with the features, and the `responses` matrix is the one with classification data. The `tflag` parameter will tell whether the features are put in rows or columns.

After that, predicting is a simple matter of creating a new row matrix with the input parameters for height, hair size, and beard presence, and passing it to the `Boost` `predict` function. Its output will classify the input as male or female:

```
public class App
{
    static{ System.loadLibrary(Core.NATIVE_LIBRARY_NAME); }

    public static void main(String[] args) throws Exception {

        Mat data = new Mat(5, 3, CvType.CV_32FC1, new Scalar(0));

        data.put(0, 0, new float[]{1.69f, 1, 0});
```

```
data.put(1, 0, new float[]{1.76f, 0, 0});
data.put(2, 0, new float[]{1.80f, 0, 0});
data.put(3, 0, new float[]{1.77f, 0, 0});
data.put(4, 0, new float[]{1.83f, 0, 1});

Mat responses = new Mat(5, 1, CvType.CV_32SC1, new Scalar(0));

responses.put(0,0, new int[]{0,1,1,0,1});



Boost boost = Boost.create();
boost.setBoostType(Boost.DISCRETE);
boost.setWeakCount(3);
boost.setMinSampleCount(4);

boost.train(data, Ml.ROW_SAMPLE, responses);

//This will simply show the input data is correctly classified

for(int i=0;i<5;i++){
  System.out.println("Result = " + boost.predict(data.row(i)));
}

Mat newPerson = new Mat(1,3,CvType.CV_32FC1, new Scalar(0));
newPerson.put(0, 0, new float[]{1.60f, 1,0});
System.out.println(newPerson.dump());
System.out.println("New (woman) = " + boost.predict(newPerson));

newPerson.put(0, 0, new float[]{1.8f, 0,1});
System.out.println("New (man) = " + boost.predict(newPerson));

newPerson.put(0, 0, new float[]{1.7f, 1,0});
System.out.println("New (?) = " + boost.predict(newPerson));

  }
}
```

Cascade classifier detection and training

One might be wondering how OpenCV could detect faces as this would be a very straightforward task for a couple-of-month old baby, and it looks quite complicated to tell a computer how to accomplish it. We will divide the problem in two parts— *object detection*, which is applying a classifier and retrieving the object position when the classifier says so, and *training* a new classifier to learn new objects that should be mostly rigid.

OpenCV Cascade Classifier initially implemented a face-detection technique known as the *Viola-Jones* detector, first developed by Paul Viola and Michael Jones, which uses the so-called Haar-like features, named after Alfréd Haar wavelets. These features are based on thresholds of sums and differences of rectangular regions of raw image values. Later, this classifier also enabled the use of **Local Binary Patterns (LBP)** features, which are integer values in contrast to Haar-like features; this results in faster training times, but similar quality.

Although using a cascade classifier in OpenCV is quite straightforward, it is important to know how it works to understand the usage boundaries. As a thumb rule, it should work fine on objects that are consistently textured and mostly rigid. The cascade classifier is presented with a set of size and histogram equalized images that are labeled as either containing or not containing an interest object. The classifier iterates through several smaller windows that cover the whole image, so it will tend to rarely find an object. For instance, group pictures will have faces in just a couple of coordinates, while the rest of the image should be labeled as not having a face. Since it should maximize rejection, the OpenCV cascade classifier uses a form of AdaBoost classifier organized as a rejection cascade, which means non-object patches should be dropped as early as possible.

Features thresholds can be used as weak classifiers to build a strong classifier using AdaBoost, as we have learned in this chapter. After we calculate a feature, we can decide on this question: *Is this value above or below a given threshold?* If the answer is `true`, the object is a face, for instance, or else it is not. We generally use a single feature for this decision, but this number can be set in training. Using AdaBoost, we build the classifier as a weighted sum of the weak classifiers like this:

$$F = sign\left(w_1 f_1 + w_2 f_2 + \ldots + w_n f_n\right)$$

Here, f_i is the function associated to each feature i, which returns +1 in case the feature value is above some threshold and -1 in case it is below. Boosting is used to correctly quantify each of the weights w_i related to the features. The Viola-Jones classifier builds each node of the tree as the signal of a weighted sum, like in the function F. Once this function is set, it yields a node for the Viola-Jones classifier, and all the surviving data from higher up in the cascade is then used to train the next node and so on. The final tree looks similar to this:

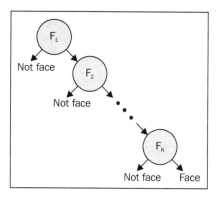

Detection

OpenCV already comes with several previously-trained cascades that are ready to be used. Among them, we can find front and profile face detectors as well as eye, body, mouth, nose, lower-body, and upper-body detectors. In this section, we will cover how to use them. The complete source can be found in the project cascade in this chapter.

The following code shows how to load a trained cascade:

```
private void loadCascade() {
    String cascadePath = "src/main/resources/cascades/lbpcascade_
frontalface.xml";
    faceDetector = new CascadeClassifier(cascadePath);
}
```

Most of the action happens in the class CascadeClassifier, from the objdetect package. This class wraps cascade loading and object detection. The constructor with strings already loads the cascade from the given path. In case you want to postpone the cascade name, you can use the empty constructor and the load method.

The `runMainLoop` method, which is not shown here, will simply grab an image from the webcam and pass it to `detectAndDrawFace`, which will put the initialized classifier to work. The following is the `detectAndDrawFace` method:

```
private void detectAndDrawFace(Mat image) {
  MatOfRect faceDetections = new MatOfRect();
  faceDetector.detectMultiScale(image, faceDetections);
  for (Rect rect : faceDetections.toArray()) {
    Core.rectangle(image, new Point(rect.x, rect.y), new Point(rect.x
+ rect.width, rect.y + rect.height), new Scalar(0, 255, 0));
  }
}
```

Firstly, we instantiate the `faceDetections` object, which is a `MatOfRect` container (a special container for `Rect`). Then, we run the `detectMultiScale` method, passing the received image and the `MatOfRect` as parameters. This is where the cascade detector is run. The algorithm will scan the image using a sliding window, running the cascade classifier for each of the windows. It will also run this procedure with different scales of the image. By default, it will reduce the image scale by 1.1 for each attempt. In case at least three detections happen, also by default, in three different scales, the coordinate is considered a hit, and it will be a part of the `faceDetections` array, added to the width and height of the detected object.

The `for` loop simply iterates through the returned rectangles and draws them in green over the original image.

Training

Although OpenCV is already packaged with several cascade classifiers, there might be a need for detecting some particular object, or class of object, of your choice. Creating a custom cascade classifier is not straightforward since it requires thousands of images from which all the variance should be removed. For instance, if a classifier for faces is being created, all the images should have their eyes aligned. In this section, we will describe the process of creating a cascade classifier using OpenCV.

In order to train a cascade, some tools have been provided in OpenCV. They can be found in the `opencv/build/x86/vc11/bin` directory. The `opencv_createsamples` and `opencv_traincascade` executables are used for preparing a training dataset of positive samples and for generating the cascade classifier, respectively.

In order to give a good idea of the process, we have included files from UIUC Image Database for Car Detection, collected by Shivani Agarwal, Aatif Awan, and Dan Roth. These files are available in the `cardata` directory from Chapter 5. The following instructions rely on being at this folder to work.

Positive samples – pictures that contain the target image

Negative samples are the arbitrary images that must not contain the object that is intended to be detected.

To create your own cascade classifier, gather hundreds of pictures of the target, making sure that these pictures show enough variance to give a good idea of the class of the object being detected.

Then, use the `opencv_createsamples` tool to prepare a training dataset of positive and test samples. This yields a binary file with the `.vec` extension, which contains positive samples generated from a given marked up dataset. No distortion is applied; they are only resized to target samples' size and stored in the `vec-file` output. The reader should issue the following command:

```
opencv_createsamples -info cars.info -num 550 -w 48 -h 24 -vec cars.
vec.
```

The preceding command will read file `cars.info`, which contains, in each line, the path to an image followed by a number n. This number is the quantity of object instances present in the image. Following this, there are n coordinates of the object bounding `rectangle (x, y, width, height)`. These are the examples of valid lines:

```
images/image1.jpg  1  90 100 45 45
images/image2.jpg  2  200 300 50 50   100 30 25 25
```

The parameters `-w` and `-h` give the width and height of the output samples that we want to be generated. This should be kept small enough so that in the image we are searching for object in the later object detection, the size of the object in the image will be greater than this size. The `-num` parameter tells the number of these samples.

In order to create a classifier for a given `.vec` file, use the `opencv_traincascade` tool. This application will read positive samples from the file given through the `-vec` parameter as well as some negative samples from a file given by the `-bg` parameter. The negative samples file simply points to an image in each of the lines, which are arbitrary ones and must not contain the object that is intended to be detected. In order to use this tool, issue the following command:

```
opencv_traincascade -data data -vec cars.vec -bg cars-neg.info -numPos
500 -numNeg 500 -numStages 10 -w 48 -h 24 -featureType LBP
```

The parameters -numPos and -numNeg are used to specify the number of positive and negative samples used in training for every classifier stage, while -numStages specifies the number of cascade stages to be trained. The last -featureType parameter sets which type of feature is to be used and can be selected from Haar-like features or LBP. As stated before, LBP features are integer values in contrast to Haar features, so detection and training will be much faster with LBP, but their quality can be the same, depending on the training. More parameters can be used to fine-tune the training, such as the false alarm rate, maximum tree depth, and minimal hit rate. The reader should refer to documentation for these settings. Now, regarding the training time, even on fast machines, it can take from a couple of hours to a few days. But, if you don't want to wait for final results, and are impatient to check how the classifier would work, you can get the intermediate classifier XML file using the following command:

```
convert_cascade --size="48x24" haarcascade haarcascade-inter.xml
```

Here 48 and 24 are the width and height for minimum possible detection and are similar to -w and -h in the opencv_traincascade command.

Once you have issued the previous command, a file called cascade.xml is created in the folder passed as the -data parameter. Other files created in this folder can be safely deleted after training has been succeeded. Now, it can be loaded and used through the CascadeClassifier class, just as described in the preceding *Detection* section. Simply use this file instead of the lbpcascade_frontalface.xml file given in that example.

The following screenshot shows one correct detection of a toy car using the trained cascade as well as one wrong detection, which is a false positive:

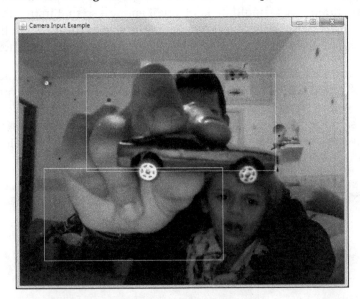

References

Refer to the video, *OpenCV Tutorial: Training your own detector*, *Packt Publishing*, (`https://www.packtpub.com/application-development/opencv-computer-vision-application-programming-video`) by Sebastian Montabone.

Summary

This chapter has provided the reader with several interesting concepts. We have covered a solid background on the boosting theory as well as working on a practical example. Then, we also covered OpenCV's Viola-Jones cascade classifier, and a hands-on approach was applied in order to use a classifier through the `CascadeClassifier` class. After that, we covered a complete, real-world example for creating a new car classifier, which can be adapted for any mostly rigid object of your preference.

In the next chapter, we will study and practice the field of background subtraction using pure image-processing methods through frame differencing and averaging background, and the interesting Kinect device for depth maps.

6
Detecting Foreground and Background Regions and Depth with a Kinect Device

In the field of video security applications, one often needs to notice the differences between frames because that's where the action happens. In other fields, it is also very important to isolate the objects from the background. This chapter shows several techniques to achieve this goal, comparing their strengths and weaknesses. Another completely different approach for detecting foreground or background regions is using a depth device like a **Kinect**. This chapter also deals with how to accomplish this goal with this device.

In this chapter, we will be covering:

- Background subtraction
- Frame differencing
- Averaging background method
- Mixture of Gaussian's method
- Contour finding
- Kinect depth maps

By the end of this chapter, you will have several approaches solving the problem of finding foreground/background regions, either through direct image processing or using a depth-compatible device such as a Kinect.

Background subtraction

When working with surveillance cameras, it's easy to see that most of the frame keeps still, while the moving objects, the ones we are interested in, are the areas that vary most over time. Background subtraction is defined as the approach used to detect moving objects from static cameras, also known as **foreground detection**, since we're mostly interested in the foreground objects.

In order to perform some valuable background subtraction, it is important to account for varying luminance conditions, taking care always to update our background model. Although some techniques extend the idea of background subtraction beyond its literal meaning, such as the mixture of Gaussian approach, they are still named like this.

In order to compare all the solutions in the following sections, we will come up with a useful interface, which is called **VideoProcessor**. This interface is made of a simple method called **process**. The whole interface is given in the following piece of code:

```
public interface VideoProcessor {
    public Mat process(Mat inputImage);
}
```

Note that we will implement this interface in the following background processors so that we can easily change them and compare their results. In this context, `Mat inputImage` refers to the current frame in the video sequence being processed.

All the code related to background subtraction can be found in the `background` project, available in the `chapter6` reference code.

Our main application consists of two windows. One of them simply plays back the input video or the webcam stream, while the other one shows the output of applying a background subtractor that implements the `VideoProcessor` interface. This way, our main loop looks pretty much like the following code:

```
while (true){
    capture.read(currentImage);
    if( !currentImage.empty() ){
        foregroundImage = videoProcessor.process(currentImage);
        ... update Graphical User Interfaces ...
        Thread.sleep(10);
    }
}
```

Note that upon successful image retrieval, we pass it to our `VideoProcessor` and update our windows. We also sleep for 10 ms so that the video playback will not look like a fast forward. This 10 ms delay is not the recorded frame delay and it is used because the focus here is not to play back at the same speed as the original file. In order to try the different subtraction approaches, we simply change the instantiation of our `VideoProcessor` class.

Frame differencing

It should be straightforward to think of a simple background subtraction in order to retrieve foreground objects. A simple solution could look similar to the following line of code:

```
Core.absdiff(backgroundImage,inputImage , foregroundImage);
```

This function simply subtracts each pixel of `backgroundImage` from `inputImage` and writes its absolute value in `foregroundImage`. As long as we have initialized the background to `backgroundImage` and we have that clear from objects, this could work as a simple solution.

Here follows the background subtraction video processor code:

```
public class AbsDifferenceBackground implements VideoProcessor {
  private Mat backgroundImage;

  public AbsDifferenceBackground(Mat backgroundImage) {
    this.backgroundImage = backgroundImage;
  }

  public Mat process(Mat inputImage) {
    Mat foregroundImage = new Mat();
    Core.absdiff(backgroundImage,inputImage , foregroundImage);
    return foregroundImage;
  }

}
```

The main method, `process`, is really simple. It only applies the absolute difference method. The only detail to remember is to initialize the background image in the constructor, which should correspond to the whole background being free from the foreground objects.

We can see the output of applying ordinary background subtraction in the following image; it is important to check that the moving leaves in the background are not correctly removed since this is a weak background modeling. Also, remember to move the **Video Playback Example** window as it might be covering the **Background Removal Example** window:

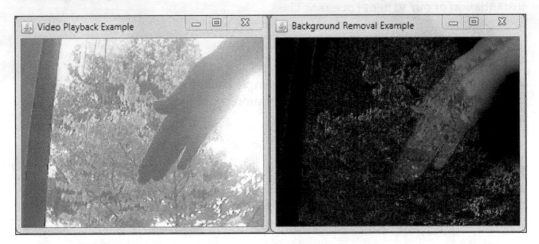

Averaging a background method

The problem with the background subtractor from the previous section is that the background will generally change due to illumination and other effects. Another fact is that the background may not be readily available, or the concept of background can change, for instance, when someone leaves a luggage in a video surveillance application. The luggage might be a foreground object for the first frames, but afterwards, it should be forgotten.

An interesting algorithm to deal with these problems uses the running average concept. Instead of always using the first frame as a clear background, it will update it constantly by calculating a moving average of it. Consider the following equation, which will be executed, updating each pixel from the old average and considering each pixel from the recently acquired image:

$$u_t = (1 - \alpha)u_{t-1} + \alpha p_t$$

Note that p_t is the new pixel value; u_{t-1} is the value of the average background at time t-1, which would be the last frame; u_t is the new value for the background; and α is the learning rate.

Fortunately, OpenCV already has the `accumulateWeighted` function, which performs the last equation for us. Now let's see how the average background process is implemented in the `RunningAverageBackground` class as we check its `process` method as follows:

```
public Mat process(Mat inputImage) {
  Mat foregroundThresh = new Mat();
  // Firstly, convert to gray-level image, yields good results with
performance
    Imgproc.cvtColor(inputImage, inputGray, Imgproc.COLOR_BGR2GRAY);
    // initialize background to 1st frame, convert to floating type
    if (accumulatedBackground.empty())
      inputGray.convertTo(accumulatedBackground, CvType.CV_32F);

    // convert background to 8U, for differencing with input image
    accumulatedBackground.convertTo(backImage,CvType.CV_8U);
    // compute difference between image and background
    Core.absdiff(backImage,inputGray,foreground);

    // apply threshold to foreground image
    Imgproc.threshold(foreground,foregroundThresh, threshold,255,
Imgproc.THRESH_BINARY_INV);

    // accumulate background
    Mat inputFloating = new Mat();
    inputGray.convertTo(inputFloating, CvType.CV_32F);
    Imgproc.accumulateWeighted(inputFloating, accumulatedBackground,lear
ningRate, foregroundThresh);

    return negative(foregroundThresh);
}

private Mat negative(Mat foregroundThresh) {
  Mat result = new Mat();
  Mat white = foregroundThresh.clone();
  white.setTo(new Scalar(255.0));
  Core.subtract(white, foregroundThresh,  result);
  return result;
}
```

First, we convert the input image to gray level since we will store the average background like this, although we could make it with three channels. Then, if the accumulated background hasn't been started, we will have to set it to the first input image in the floating point format. Then we subtract the recently acquired frame from the accumulated background, which yields our foreground image, which we later threshold in order to remove small illumination or noisy changes.

Note that this time we use `Imgproc.THRESH_BINARY_INV`, which turns every pixel above the given threshold black, yielding black pixels for the foreground objects and white pixels for the background.

This way, we can use this image as a mask for updating only background pixels when using the `acccumulateWeighted` method later. On the following line, we only convert `inputImage` to `inputFloating` so that we can have it in the floating point format. We then use `accumulateWeighted` to apply our commented equation for the running average. Finally, we invert the image and return our foreground objects as white pixels.

We can see a better modeling of the moving leaves on the background in the following image. Although thresholding makes it harder to compare these results with simple background subtraction, it is clear that lots of moving leaves have been removed. Besides, a good part of the hand has also been swept away. A careful tuning of the threshold parameter can be used for better results as shown in the following screenshot:

The mixture of Gaussians method

Although we can get very good results with the previous idea, some more advanced methods have been proposed in literature. A great approach, proposed by Grimson in 1999, is to use not just one running average, but more averages so that if a pixel fluctuates between the two orbit points, these two running averages are calculated. If it does not fit any of them, it is considered foreground.

Besides, Grimson's approach also keeps the variance of the pixels, which is a measure of how far a set of numbers is spread out, taken from statistics. With a mean and a variance, a Gaussian model can be calculated and a probability can be measured to be taken into consideration, yielding a **Mixture of Gaussians model (MOG)**. This can be very useful when branches and leaves are moving in the background.

Unfortunately, Grimson's method suffers from slow learning in the beginning and it can not distinguish between the moving shadows and moving objects. Therefore, an improved technique has been published by KaewTraKulPong and Bowden to tackle these problems. This one is implemented in OpenCV and it is quite straightforward to use it by means of the `BackgroundSubtractorMOG2` class.

In order to show how effective is the mixture of Gaussians approach, we have implemented a `BackgroundSubtractorMOG2`-based `VideoProcessor`. Its entire code is as follows:

```
public class MixtureOfGaussianBackground implements VideoProcessor {
  privateBackgroundSubtractorMOG2 mog=  org.opencv.video.Video.
    createBackgroundSubtractorMOG2();
  private Mat foreground = new Mat();
  private double learningRate = 0.01;

  public Mat process(Mat inputImage) {
    mog.apply(inputImage, foreground, learningRate);
    return foreground;
  }
}
```

Note that we only need to instantiate the `BackgroundSubtractorMOG2` class and use the `apply` method, passing the input frame, the output image, and a learning rate that will tell how fast it should learn the new background. Besides the factory method without parameters, another one exists with the following signature:

```
Video.createBackgroundSubtractorMOG2 (int history, double
varThreshold, boolean detectShadows)
```

Here, `history` is the length of the history, `varThreshold` is the threshold on the squared Mahalanobis distance between the pixel and the model to decide whether a pixel is well described by the background model, and if `detectShadows` is `true`, the algorithm will detect and mark the shadows. If we do not set parameters by using the empty constructor, the following values are used by default:

- `defaultHistory = 500;`
- `varThreshold = 16;`
- `detectShadows = true;`

Try playing with these values in order to look for better results when making background subtraction.

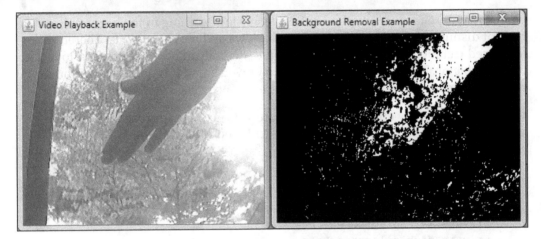

In the preceding screenshot, we can clearly see a great background removal result with very little customization. Although some leaves still account for noise in the removed background result, we can see a good amount of the hand being correctly identified as foreground. A simple open morphological operator can be applied to remove some of the noise, as seen in the following screenshot:

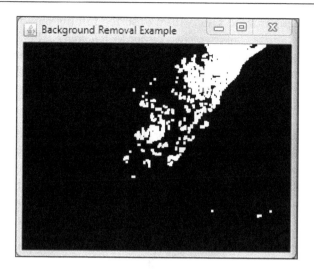

Contour finding

When dealing with the binary images removed from the background, it is important to transform pixels into useful information, such as by grouping them into an object or making it very clear for the user to see. In this context, it is important to know the concept of connected components, which are a set of connected pixels in a binary image, and OpenCV's function used to find its contours.

In this section, we will examine the findContours function, which extracts contours of connected components in an image as well as a helper function that will draw contours in an image, which is drawContours. The findContours function is generally applied over an image that has gone through a threshold procedure as well as some canny image transformation. In our example, a threshold is used.

The findContours function has the following signature:

```
public static void findContours(Mat image,
                java.util.List<MatOfPoint> contours,
                Mat hierarchy,
                int mode,
                int method)
```

It is implemented using Suzuki's algorithm described in his paper *Topological structural analysis of digitized binary images by border following*. The first parameter is the input image. Make sure you work on a copy of your target image since this function alters the image. Also, beware that the 1 pixel border of the image is not considered. The contours that are found are stored in the list of `MatOfPoints`. This is simply a structure that stores points in a matrix.

`Mat hierarchy` is an optional output vector that is set for each contour found. They represent 0-based indices of the next and previous contours at the same hierarchical level, the first child contour, and the parent contour, represented in the `hierarcy[i] [0]`, `hierarcy[i][1]`, `hierarcy[i][2]`, and `hierarcy[i][3]` elements, respectively for a given `i` contour. If there aren't contours corresponding to those values, they will be negative.

The `mode` parameter deals with how the hierarchical relationships are established. If this is not interesting to you, you can set it as `Imgproc.RETR_LIST`. When retrieving the contours, the `method` parameter controls how they are approximated. If `Imgproc.CHAIN_APPROX_NONE` is set, all the contour points are stored. On the other hand, when using `Imgproc.CHAIN_APPROX_SIMPLE` for this value, horizontal, vertical, and diagonal lines are compressed by using only their endpoints. Other approximations are available as well.

In order to draw the obtained contours outline or fill them, Imgproc's `drawContours` is used. This function has the following signature:

```
public static void drawContours(Mat image,
                java.util.List<MatOfPoint> contours,
                int contourIdx,
                Scalar color)
```

`Mat image` is simply the destination image, while the list of `MatOfPoint` contours is the one obtained while calling `findContours`. The `contourIdx` property is the one intended to be drawn, while `color` is the desired color for drawing. Overloaded functions are also available in which the user can choose the thickness, line type, hierarchy max level, and an offset.

When deciding on which contours are interesting, a useful function to help in that decision is to find the contour area. OpenCV implements this function through `Imgproc.contourArea`. This function can be found in the `chapter6` source code's sample `connected` project. This application takes an image as input, runs a threshold over it and then uses it for finding the contours. Several options are available for testing the functions discussed in this section, such as whether it is filling the contour or painting the contour according to the area found. The following is a screenshot of this application:

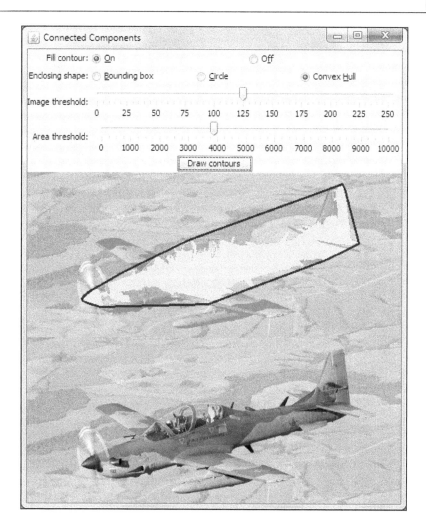

When dealing with contours, it is also important to draw shapes around them in order to make measures or highlight what is found. The sample application also offers some code with instructions on how to draw a bounding box, circle, or convex hull around the contour. Let's take a look at the main `drawContours()` function, which is called upon pressing the button:

```
protected void drawContours() {
  Mat contourMat = binary.clone();
  List<MatOfPoint> contours = new ArrayList<MatOfPoint>();
  int thickness = (fillFlag.equals(onFillString))?-1:2;

  Imgproc.findContours(contourMat, contours, new Mat(),
  Imgproc.CHAIN_APPROX_NONE,Imgproc.CHAIN_APPROX_SIMPLE);
```

```
for(int i=0;i<contours.size();i++){
    MatOfPoint currentContour = contours.get(i);
    double currentArea = Imgproc.contourArea(currentContour);

    if(currentArea > areaThreshold){
        Imgproc.drawContours(image, contours, i, new Scalar(0,255,0),
thickness);
        if(boundingBoxString.equals(enclosingType)){
            drawBoundingBox(currentContour);
        }
        else if (circleString.equals(enclosingType)){
        drawEnclosingCircle(currentContour);
        }
        else if (convexHullString.equals(enclosingType)){
            drawConvexHull(currentContour);
        }
    }
    else{
        Imgproc.drawContours(image, contours, i, new Scalar(0,0,255),
thickness);
    }
}
updateView();
}
```

We firstly clone our target binary image, so we won't change it. Then, we initialize the `MatOfPoint` structure and define the thickness flag. We then run `findContours`, ignoring the output hierarchy matrix. It is time to iterate the contours in the `for` loop. We use the `Imgproc.contourArea` helper function for an area estimate. Based on that, if it is the previous `areaThreshold` defined by the slider, it is drawn as green using the `drawContours` function or else it is drawn as red. An interesting part of the code are the shape drawing functions, which are described as follows:

```
private void drawBoundingBox(MatOfPoint currentContour) {
    Rect rectangle = Imgproc.boundingRect(currentContour);
    Imgproc.rectangle(image, rectangle.tl(), rectangle.br(), new
Scalar(255,0,0),1);
}

private void drawEnclosingCircle(MatOfPoint currentContour) {
    float[] radius = new float[1];
    Point center = new Point();

    MatOfPoint2f currentContour2f = new MatOfPoint2f();
    currentContour.convertTo(currentContour2f, CvType.CV_32FC2);
```

```
        Imgproc.minEnclosingCircle(currentContour2f, center, radius);
        Imgproc.circle(image, center, (int) radius[0], new Scalar(255,0,0));
    }

    private void drawConvexHull(MatOfPoint currentContour) {
        MatOfInt hull = new MatOfInt();
        Imgproc.convexHull(currentContour, hull);

        List<MatOfPoint> hullContours = new ArrayList<MatOfPoint>();
        MatOfPoint hullMat = new MatOfPoint();
        hullMat.create((int)hull.size().height,1,CvType.CV_32SC2);

        for(int j = 0; j < hull.size().height ; j++){
            int index = (int)hull.get(j, 0)[0];
            double[] point = new double[] {
                currentContour.get(index, 0)[0], currentContour.get(index, 0)[1]
            };
            hullMat.put(j, 0, point);
        }
        hullContours.add(hullMat);
        Imgproc.drawContours(image, hullContours, 0, new Scalar(128,0,0),
    2);
    }
```

Drawing a bounding box is simple; it is just a matter of calling `Imgproc.boundingRect()` in order to identify the shape's surrounding rectangle. Then, the Imgproc's `rectangle` function method is called to draw the rectangle itself.

Drawing the enclosing circle is also easy due to the existence of the `minEnclosingCircle` function. The only caveat is converting `MatOfPoint` to `MatOfPoint2f`, which is accomplished by calling Contour's `convertTo`. The Imgproc's `circle` function deals with drawing it.

Finding the convex hull is a rather important problem from a computational geometry perspective. It can be seen as putting an elastic band around a set of points and checking the final shape it takes. Fortunately, OpenCV also deals with this problem through the Imgproc's `convexHull` function. Note that in the first and the second line of `drawConvexHull` in the preceding code, `MatOfInt` is created, and `convexHull` is called, passing the current contour and this matrix as parameters. This function will return convex hull indexes in `MatOfInt`. We can draw lines ourselves, based on the coordinates of these indexes from the original contour. Another idea is to use the OpenCV's `drawContour` function. In order to do this, you need to build a new contour. This is done in the following lines in the code until `drawContour` is called.

Kinect depth maps

From the beginning of this chapter until now, we have focused on the background subtraction approaches that try to model the background of the scene using ordinary cameras and then on applying frame differencing.

 Although the Kinect is reported to work with Linux and OSX, this section deals only with Windows setup on OpenCV 2.4.7 version.

In this section, we will take a different approach. We will set how far we want our objects to be considered foreground and background, which means removing the background by selecting a depth parameter. Unfortunately, this can not be done using a single ordinary camera in a single shot, so we will need a sensor that tells us the depth of objects or try to determine depth from stereo, which is not in the scope of this chapter. Thanks to both gamers and several efforts from all around the world, this device has become a commodity and it is called a **Kinect**. Some attempts can be made to use two cameras and try to get depth from stereo, but the results might not be as great as the ones with the Kinect sensor. Here is how it looks:

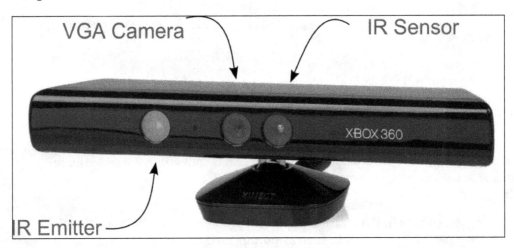

What makes the Kinect really different from an average camera is that it includes an infrared emitter and an infrared sensor that are able to project and sense a structured light pattern. It also contains an ordinary VGA camera so that the depth data can be merged into it. The idea behind the structured light is that when projecting a known pattern of pixels on to the objects, the deformation of this pattern allows the computer vision systems to calculate the depth and surface information from them. If a camera capable of registering infrared is used to record the emitted Kinect pattern, an image similar to the following can be seen:

Although it might look like a random set of points, they are actually pseudo-random patterns that have been previously generated. These patterns can be identified and a disparity to depth relationship can be calculated, inferring the depth. More information can be acquired when studying structured light concepts if it is required.

One should be aware of the implications this method has. As it relies on active infrared projection, some outdoor effects, such as direct sunlight will confuse the sensors, so outdoor use is not recommended. Users should also be aware that the depth range is from 0.8 meters to 4.0 meters (roughly from 2.6 feet to 13.1 feet). Some shadows related to the IR projection can also make the results not look as great as they should, and cause some noise in the images. Despite all these issues, it is one of the best results available for the near field background removal.

The Kinect setup

Using a Kinect should be straightforward, but we need to consider two important aspects. First we need to be sure that all the device driver softwares are correctly installed for using them. Then we need to check whether OpenCV has been compiled with Kinect support. Unfortunately, if you have downloaded precompiled binaries of version 2.4.7 from `http://sourceforge.net/projects/opencvlibrary/files/`, as described in the beginning of *Chapter 1, Setting Up OpenCV for Java* the out-of-the-box support is not included. We will briefly describe the setup instructions in the upcoming sections.

It is important to note that not only the Xbox 360 Kinect device is commercialized, but also the Kinect for Windows. Currently, if you are creating commercial applications with the Kinect, you should go with the Kinect for Windows, although the Xbox 360 Kinect works with the provided drivers.

The driver setup

OpenCV Kinect support relies on OpenNI and PrimeSensor Module for OpenNI. An OpenNI framework is an open source SDK used for the development of 3D sensing middleware libraries and applications. Unfortunately, `OpenNI.org` site was available only until April 23rd, 2014, but the OpenNI source code is available on Github at `https://github.com/OpenNI/OpenNI` and `https://github.com/OpenNI/OpenNI2`. We will focus on using version 1.5.7.10 in this section.

Although instructions for building the binaries are readily available, we can use installers provided in the code repository of this book.

After installing the OpenNI library, we will need to install the Kinect drivers. These are available at `https://github.com/avin2/SensorKinect/`, and installers are specifically at `https://github.com/avin2/SensorKinect/tree/unstable/Bin`.

When plugging your Xbox 360 Kinect device into Windows, you should see the following screenshot in your Device Manager:

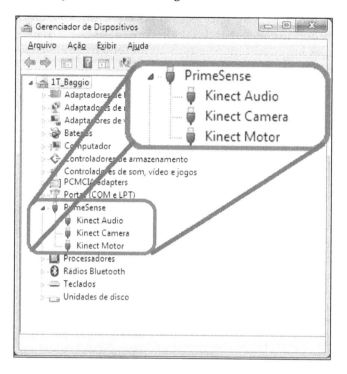

Make sure all of the three Kinect devices — **Audio**, **Camera**, and **Motor** — show appropriately.

 One caveat that can happen is that if users forget to plug the power supply for the XBox 360 Kinect device, only **Kinect Motor** might show up since there isn't enough energy for the all three of them. Also, you won't be able to retrieve frames in your OpenCV application. Remember to plugin your power supply, and you should be fine.

The OpenCV Kinect support

After ensuring that the OpenNI and Kinect drivers have been correctly installed, you need to check for the OpenCV Kinect support. Fortunately, OpenCV offers quite a useful function to check that. It is called `Core.getBuildInformation()`. This function shows important information about which options have been enabled during the OpenCV compilation. In order to check for Kinect support, simply output the result of calling this function to the console by using `System.out.println(Core.getBuildInformation());` and look for the video I/O section which looks like the following:

```
Video I/O:
        Video for Windows:              YES
        DC1394 1.x:                     NO
        DC1394 2.x:                     NO
        FFMPEG:                         YES (prebuilt binaries)
          codec:                        YES (ver 55.18.102)
          format:                       YES (ver 55.12.100)
          util:                         YES (ver 52.38.100)
          swscale:                      YES (ver 2.3.100)
          gentoo-style:                 YES
        OpenNI:                         NO
        OpenNI PrimeSensor Modules:     NO
        PvAPI:                          NO
        GigEVisionSDK:                  NO
        DirectShow:                     YES
        Media Foundation:               NO
        XIMEA:                          NO
```

It means OpenNI and Kinect support has not been enabled.

1. Now, according to *Chapter 1*, *Setting Up OpenCV for Java*, instead of typing:

   cmake -DBUILD_SHARED_LIBS=OFF ..

   Remember to add the `WITH_OPENNI` flag, as given in the following line of code:

   ```
   cmake -DBUILD_SHARED_LIBS=OFF .. -D WITH_OPENNI
   ```

Instead of the preceding code, make sure you tick this option when using CMake's GUI. Check for an output similar to the following screenshot:

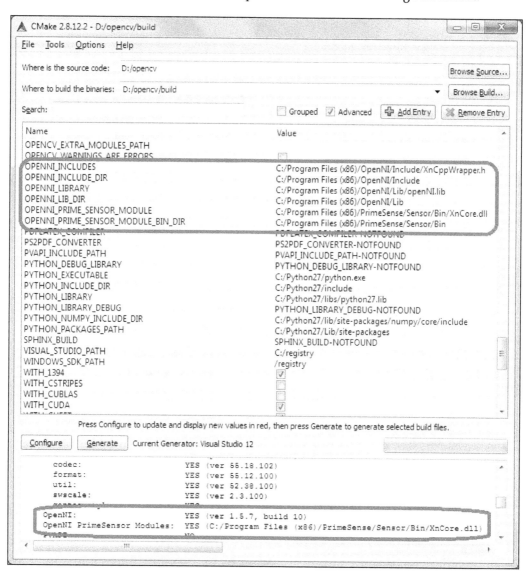

Make sure you point the OPENNI paths to your OpenNI correct installation folder. Rebuild the library, and now your `opencv_java247.dll` will be built with Kinect support.

2. Now try checking your `Core.getBuildInformation()` again. The availability of OpenNI will be demonstrated in your Java console, as given in the following lines:

```
Video I/O:
   Video for Windows:          YES
   DC1394 1.x:                 NO
   DC1394 2.x:                 NO
   FFMPEG:                     YES (prebuilt binaries)
     codec:                    YES (ver 55.18.102)
     format:                   YES (ver 55.12.100)
     util:                     YES (ver 52.38.100)
     swscale:                  YES (ver 2.3.100)
     gentoo-style:             YES
   OpenNI:                     YES (ver 1.5.7, build 10)
   OpenNI PrimeSensor Modules: YES (C:/Program Files (x86)/
PrimeSense/Sensor/Bin/XnCore.dll)
   PvAPI:                      NO
   GigEVisionSDK:              NO
   DirectShow:                 YES
   Media Foundation:           NO
   XIMEA:                      NO
```

An alternative approach is using our configured Maven repository. We have added a runtime dependency to the book Maven repository, only available for Windows x86, which is very easy to configure. Simply follow the Java OpenCV Maven configuration section from *Chapter 1, Setting Up OpenCV for Java*, and then, instead of adding the ordinary OpenCV dependency, `opencvjar-runtime`, use the following dependency:

```xml
<dependency>
  <groupId>org.javaopencvbook</groupId>
  <artifactId>opencvjar-kinect-runtime</artifactId>
  <version>2.4.7</version>
  <classifier>natives-windows-x86</classifier>
</dependency>
```

The complete POM file can be accessed in this chapter's Kinect project source code.

Be sure you check for some caveats, such as not mixing 32 bit and 64 bit drivers and libraries as well as Java runtime. If this is the case, you might receive **Can't load IA 32-bit .dll on a AMD 64-bit platform**, for instance. Another source of problems is forgetting to plugin the power supply for Kinect XBox 360, which will cause it to load only Kinect Motor.

Now that we are sure that the OpenNI and Kinect Drivers have been correctly installed as well as the OpenCV's OpenNI support, we are ready to move on to the next section.

The Kinect depth application

The application focuses on the depth-sensing information from the Kinect as well as on the OpenCV API for OpenNI depth sensor, which means it won't cover some well-known Kinect features such as skeletal tracking (which puts nodes in important body parts like head, heap center, shoulder, wrists, hands, knees, feet, and others), gesture tracking, microphone recording, or tilting the device. Although we will just cover depth sensing, it is one of the most fantastic features of the Kinect.

The basic idea behind this application is to segment an image from its depth information and combine it with a background image. We will capture an RGB frame from the Kinect device and retrieve its depth map. From a slider, you can choose how much depth you want for the segmentation. Based on that, a mask is generated through simple thresholding. The combined RGB frame and depth are now used to overlay a background image, resulting in an effect similar to chroma key compositing, but without the need for a green screen background, of course. This process can be seen in the following screenshot:

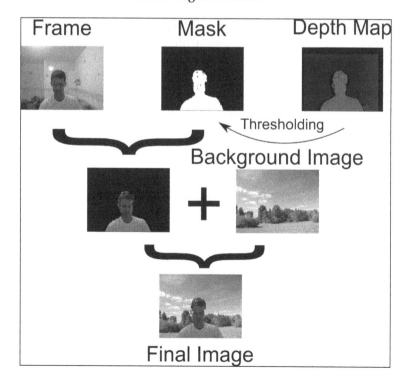

We should notice that in OpenCV version 2.4.7, the Java API does not support the Kinect depth sensing, but this is built on top of `VideoCapture`, so just some minor modifications related to constants will be required. For the sake of simplicity, these constants are in the main `App` class, but they should be refactored to a class that only deals with the OpenNI constants. Please look for the project `kinect` from this chapter in order to check for source code.

In order to work with depth-sensing images, we will need to follow these simple guidelines:

```
VideoCapture capture = new VideoCapture(CV_CAP_OPENNI);
capture.grab();
capture.retrieve( depthMap,  CV_CAP_OPENNI_DEPTH_MAP);
capture.retrieve(colorImage, CV_CAP_OPENNI_BGR_IMAGE);
```

We will use the same `VideoCapture` class as the one used in *Chapter 2, Handling Matrices, Files, Cameras, and GUIs,* for webcam input, with the same interface, passing the constant `CV_CAP_OPENNI` for telling it to retrieve frames from the Kinect. The difference here is that instead of using the `read` method, we will break this step in grabbing the frame and then retrieving either the depth image or the captured frame. Note that this is done by firstly calling the `grab` method and then the `retrieve` method, passing `CV_CAP_OPENNI_DEPTH_MAP` and `CV_CAP_OPENNI_BGR_IMAGE` as parameters. Make sure you send it to different matrices. Note that all these constants are extracted from the `highgui_c.h` file, which is located in the `opencv\modules\highgui\include\opencv2\highgui` path from OpenCV's source code tree. We will only work with the disparity map and RGB images from the Kinect, but one can also use the `CV_CAP_OPENNI_DEPTH_MAP` constant for receiving the depth values in mm as a `CV_16UC1` matrix, or `CV_CAP_OPENNI_POINT_CLOUD_MAP` for a point cloud map in a `CV_32FC3` matrix in which the values are XYZ coordinates in meters.

Our main loop consists of the following code:

```
while(true){
  capture.grab();
  capture.retrieve( depthMap, CV_CAP_OPENNI_DISPARITY_MAP);
  disparityImage = depthMap.clone();
  capture.retrieve(colorImage, CV_CAP_OPENNI_BGR_IMAGE);
  workingBackground = resizedBackground.clone();
  Imgproc.threshold(disparityImage, disparityThreshold, gui.
getLevel(), 255.0f, Imgproc.THRESH_BINARY);
  maskedImage.setTo(new Scalar(0,0,0));
  colorImage.copyTo(maskedImage,disparityThreshold);
  maskedImage.copyTo(workingBackground,maskedImage);
  renderOutputAccordingToMode(disparityImage, disparityThreshold,
  colorImage, resizedBackground, workingBackground, gui);
}
```

First, we invoke the `grab` method to get the next frame from the Kinect. Then, we retrieve depth map and color images. As we have previously loaded our background in `resizedBackground`, we just clone it to `workingBackground`. Following this, we threshold our disparity image according to our slider level. This will make pixels farther away from our desired depth go black, while the ones we still want become white. It is time to clear our mask and combine it with the colored image.

Summary

This chapter has really covered several areas that deal with background removal as well as some details that arise from this problem, such as the need to use connected components to find their contours. Firstly, the problem of background removal itself was established. Then, a simple algorithm such as frame differencing was analyzed. After that, more interesting algorithms, such as averaging background and **mixture of Gaussian (MOG)** were covered.

After using algorithms to deal with background removal problems, an insight about connected components was explored. Core OpenCV algorithms such as `findContours` and `drawContours` were explained. Some properties of contours were also analyzed, such as their area as well as convex hulls.

The chapter finished with complete explanations of how to use the Kinect's depth sensor device as a background removal tool, for OpenCV 2.4.7. After depth instructions on the device setup, a complete application was developed, making it clear to deal with the depth sensing sensors API.

Well, now it's time to jump from desktop applications to web apps in the next chapter. There, we'll cover details on how to set up an OpenCV-based web application, deal with image uploads, and create a nice augmented reality application based on the Tomcat web server. It is going to be fun, just watch out for Einstein's screenshots.

OpenCV on the Server Side

7

As the Internet gets more and more interactive, a subject of great interest is how to deal with image processing on the server side that enables you to create web applications dealing with OpenCV. As Java is among the languages of choice when developing web apps, this chapter shows the entire architecture of an application that lets users upload an image and add a fedora hat on top of detected faces using techniques learned throughout the book.

In this chapter, we will cover the following topics:

- Setting up an OpenCV web application
- Mixed reality
- Image uploading
- Dealing with HTTP requests

By the end of this chapter you will know how to create a complete web application with image processing, obtain input from the user, process the image on the server side, and return the processed image to the user.

Setting up an OpenCV web application

Since this chapter covers the development of a web application using Java OpenCV, it is important to address a couple of differences when going to the server side. The first thing is to tell the web container, generally Tomcat, Jetty, JBoss, or Websphere, about the location of native libraries. Other details deal with loading the native code. This should happen as soon as the web server goes up and should not occur again.

The advantages of using the web architecture are significant. As certain image-processing tasks are compute intensive, they could easily drain the device's battery in no time, so, taking them to a more robust hardware on the cloud would relieve local processing. Besides that, there's no need for users to install anything more than the web browser, and the updates happening on the server side are also very handy.

On the other hand, there are a few drawbacks. If, instead of hosting the web application on the administrator infrastructure, one intends to host it on Java servers online, it should be clear whether it allows native code to be run or not. At the time of writing, Google's App Engine does not allow it, but it is easy to set up a Linux server on Amazon EC2 or Google's Compute Engine that smoothly runs it although this won't be covered in this book. Another thing to be considered is that several computer vision applications need to be run in real time, even at the rate of 20 frames per second, for instance, which would be impractical in a web architecture, due to long upload times, and this type of application should be run locally.

In order to create our web application, we will go through the following steps:

1. Creating a Maven-based web application.
2. Adding OpenCV dependencies.
3. Running the web application.
4. Importing the project to Eclipse.

In the following sections, we will cover these steps in detail.

Creating a Maven-based web application

There are several ways to create web applications in Java. Spring MVC, Apache Wicket, and Play Framework are all great options among others. Also, on top of these frameworks, we can put JavaServer Faces, PrimeFaces, or RichFaces as component-based user interfaces for these web applications. For this chapter though, instead of addressing all these technologies, the approach will be to only use servlets for you to choose your frameworks. You should notice that a servlet is simply a Java class used to extend the capabilities of a server, and this is generally used to process or store data that was submitted through an HTML form. The servlet API has been around since 1997, so it has been exhaustively used, and there are several books and samples about it. Although this chapter focuses on Servlet 2.x for simplicity, we need to be aware that the API is synchronous and that it might be better to use an asynchronous one, such as Servlet 3.x, for applications that will receive several clients together.

Although any IDE can easily generate a web application through a wizard — such as going to Eclipse and navigating to **File | New | Project... | Web | Dynamic Web Project** — we'll focus on starting it with the help of Maven since we can easily get native dependencies. As long as it has been installed correctly according to instructions in *Chapter 1, Setting Up OpenCV for Java*, Maven can set up a web application through the use of a prototype. This is achieved through the following command:

```
mvn archetype:generate -DgroupId=com.mycompany.app -DartifactId=my-webapp
-DarchetypeArtifactId=maven-archetype-webapp -DinteractiveMode=false
```

This command will call the `generate` goal from the `archetype` plugin. Think of `archetype` as a project template. This Maven plugin will generate a web application from a template because we have set `archetypeArtifactId` as `maven-archetype-webapp` through the `-DarchetypeArtifactId=maven-archetype-webapp` option. The other option, `DartifactId=my-webapp`, will simply set the folder name of the web application as defined in this option, while `groupId` is Maven's universally unique identifier for a project.

Note that the following structure will be created:

```
my-webapp
|-- pom.xml
`-- src
    `-- resources
    `-- main
        `-- webapp
            |-- WEB-INF
            |   `-- web.xml
            `-- index.jsp
```

The preceding is a simple structure for a web application. You should pay attention to the `web.xml` file, which is used for mapping servlets, as well as `index.jsp`, which is a simple Java Server Page file. By now you should be able to run this web application in Tomcat, for instance, with little effort. Simply type the following command:

```
cd my-webapp
```

```
mvn tomcat:run
```

Now, if the you access the address `http://localhost:8080/my-webapp/`, the following response should be seen in the browser:

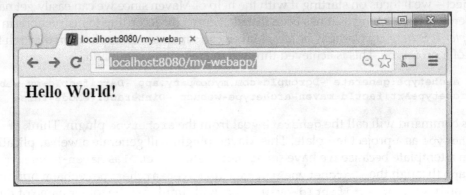

Notice that it means that we have successfully created a web project, we are running it through a Tomcat web container, and it is available through `localhost` server, in port `8080`, through the name `my-webapp`. The `Hello World!` message can be seen in `index.jsp`. In the following section, you are going to customize the `pom` file in order to add OpenCV dependencies.

Adding OpenCV dependencies

Since the web application archetype has created a project structure for us, we are going to add OpenCV dependencies for the generated `pom.xml`. If you open it, you will see the following code:

```
<project xmlns="http://maven.apache.org/POM/4.0.0" xmlns:xsi="http://
www.w3.org/2001/XMLSchema-instance"
  xsi:schemaLocation="http://maven.apache.org/POM/4.0.0 http://maven.
apache.org/maven-v4_0_0.xsd">
  <modelVersion>4.0.0</modelVersion>
  <groupId>com.mycompany.app</groupId>
  <artifactId>my-webapp</artifactId>
  <packaging>war</packaging>
  <version>1.0-SNAPSHOT</version>
  <name>my-webapp Maven Webapp</name>
  <url>http://maven.apache.org</url>
  <dependencies>
    <dependency>
      <groupId>junit</groupId>
```

```
      <artifactId>junit</artifactId>
      <version>3.8.1</version>
      <scope>test</scope>
    </dependency>
  </dependencies>
  <build>
    <finalName>my-webapp</finalName>
  </build>
</project>
```

Notice that the only dependency is on `junit`. Now add the following to the dependencies tag:

```
<dependency>
    <groupId>org.javaopencvbook</groupId>
    <artifactId>opencvjar</artifactId>
    <version>3.0.0</version>
</dependency>

<dependency>
    <groupId>org.javaopencvbook</groupId>
    <artifactId>opencvjar-runtime</artifactId>
    <version>3.0.0</version>
    <classifier>natives-windows-x86</classifier>
</dependency>

<dependency>
    <groupId>javax.servlet</groupId>
    <artifactId>javax.servlet-api</artifactId>
    <version>3.0.1</version>
    <scope>provided</scope>
</dependency>
```

The first two dependencies, `opencvjar` and `opencvjar-runtime`, are the same ones that have been discussed in *Chapter 1, Setting Up OpenCV for Java*. Now, the dependency on `javax.servlet-api` refers to the servlet API version 3.0.1, which is used to make files upload more easily. Besides using these dependencies, all other configurations are mentioned in *Chapter 1, Setting Up OpenCV for Java*, such as adding the `JavaOpenCVBook` repository, `maven-jar-plugin`, `maven-dependency-plugin`, and `maven-nativedependencies-plugin`.

The only new plugin is `tomcat7` as we would require it to use the file upload API from `servlet 3.0`. In order to add the `tomcat7` plugin, look for the `<plugins>` section in `pom.xml` and add the following code:

```
<plugin>
  <groupId>org.apache.tomcat.maven</groupId>
  <artifactId>tomcat7-maven-plugin</artifactId>
  <version>2.2</version>
  <configuration>
    <port>9090</port>
    <path>/</path>
  </configuration>
</plugin>
```

Besides adding the ability to run `tomcat7` from Maven, it will also configure port `9090` as the default port for our server, but you can use another one. The final `pom. xml` file can be found in this chapter's source code project. Running an `mvn package` command will show that everything's been fine in the project setup. In the next section, we are going to check all the processes through a simple OpenCV call from the `.jsp` file.

Running the web application

Now that all the dependencies have been set up, it should be straightforward to run our web application. One detail should be noticed, though. Since our application relies on native code, the `opencv_java300.dll` file, or the shared object, we should put it in the Java library path prior to running the Tomcat server. There are several approaches to doing this, depending on your deployment strategy, but a simple one could be setting the path through the `MAVEN_OPTS` environment variable. You should type the following command in the terminal:

```
set MAVEN_OPTS=-Djava.library.path=D:/your_path/my-webapp/target/natives
```

Please remember to change `your_path` to the place you are setting up your project, the parent folder of `my-webapp`. In order to check that the application server can correctly load OpenCV native libraries, we are going to set up a simple servlet which is able to output the correct installed version. Change the `index.jsp` file generated in your `my-webapp\src\main\webapp` folder to the following code:

```html
<html>
  <body>
    <h2>OpenCV Webapp Working!</h2>
    <%@ page import = "org.opencv.core.Core" %>
    Core.VERSION: <%= Core.VERSION %>
  </body>
</html>
```

Now, run your server typing `mvn tomcat7:run`. Try loading your application in your web browser at the address `http://localhost:9090`, and you should see the page outputting your loaded OpenCV version. Although this code doesn't really load native libraries, since `Core.VERSION` can be retrieved from pure Java JAR, it's not a good practice to mix business code — the one that really does your image processing — with your presentation code, that is, the Java Server Page we just edited. In order to deal with image processing, we are going to concentrate the code in a servlet that only deals with it.

Importing the project to Eclipse

Now that the project is all set up with Maven, it should be easy to import it to Eclipse. Simply issue the following Maven command:

```
mvn eclipse:eclipse -Dwtpversion=2.0
```

Remember to add the `-Dwtpversion=2.0` flag to add support for WTP version 2.0, which is Eclipse's Web Tools platform. If you have not set up your `M2_REPO` as explained in *Chapter 1, Setting Up OpenCV for Java*, a simple trick can automate it for you. Type the following command:

```
mvn -Declipse.workspace="YOUR_WORKSPACE_PATH" eclipse:configure-workspace
```

The `YOUR_WORKSPACE_PATH` path should be changed to something similar to `C:\Users\baggio\workspace` if that is where your Eclipse workspace is located.

In Eclipse, navigate through **File** | **Import** | **General** | **Existing Projects** into the workspace and point to your my-webapp folder. Notice that your Eclipse should have WTP support. In case you receive a Java compiler level does not match the version of the installed Java project facet message, simply right-click it and in the **Quick Fix** menu, choose **Change Java Project Facet version to Java 1.8**. Now you can run it by right-clicking in your project, navigating to **Run as** | **Run on Server**, selecting **Apache** | **Tomcat v7.0 Server**, and hitting **Next**. If you don't have an existing Tomcat 7 installation, select **Download and Install**, as shown in the next screenshot:

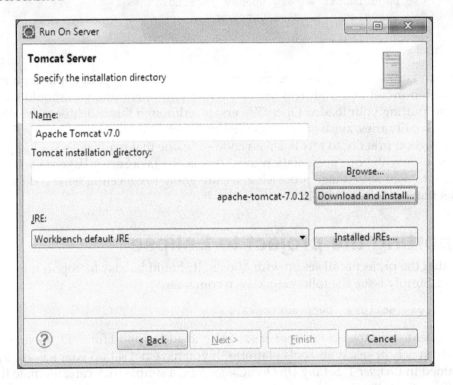

Select a folder for your Tomcat7 installation and click on **Next** and **Finish**. Now, you can run your application directly from Eclipse, by right-clicking on your project and clicking on **Run as** | **Run on Server**. In case you receive a "java.lang. UnsatisfiedLinkError: no opencv_java300 in java.library.path", right-click your project, "Run As ->Run Configurations..." and in the Arguments tab, in the VM arguments text box, add the -Djava.library.path="C:\path_to_your\target\natives". Click in "Apply" and restart your server by going to the Server tab and right-clicking your Tomcat7 execution -> Restart.

Mixed reality web applications

The web application we are going to develop draws Fedora hats on top of the detected heads in a given image. In order to do this, the user uploads the image through a simple form, and then it is converted to an OpenCV matrix in memory. After conversion, a cascade classifier looking for faces is run over the matrix. A simple scale and a translation are applied to estimate the hat's position and scale. A transparent fedora image is then drawn on the specified position for each of the detected faces. The result is then returned through HTTP by giving the mixed reality picture to the user. Notice that all the processing happens on the server side, so the client is only left to upload and download the image, which is very useful for clients that rely on batteries, such as smartphones.

Mixed reality (MR), sometimes referred to as hybrid reality (encompassing both augmented reality and augmented virtuality), refers to the merging of real and virtual worlds to produce new environments and visualisations where physical and digital objects co-exist and interact in real time. Not taking place only in the physical world or the virtual world, but a mix of reality and virtual reality, encompassing augmented reality and augmented virtuality.

Source: Fleischmann, Monika; Strauss, Wolfgang (eds.) (2001). Proceedings of »CAST01//Living in Mixed Realities« Intl. Conf. On Communication of Art, Science and Technology, Fraunhofer IMK 2001, 401. ISSN 1618–1379 (Print), ISSN 1618–1387 (Internet).

This web application can be divided into a couple of simpler steps:

1. Image upload.
2. Image processing.
3. Response image.

The following sections will cover these steps in detail.

Image upload

Firstly, we are going to turn our dummy Java Server Page into a form that will require the user to choose a local file, similar to the one seen in the following screenshot:

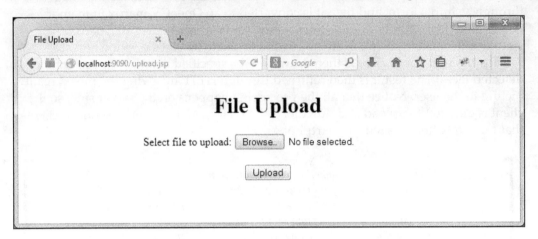

The following code shows the complete Java Server Page. Note the form element, which states that it will call a post method being processed in the doPost part of the servlet and requests that the web server to accept the data enclosed in the form for storage. The enctype= "multipart/form-data" states that no characters are going to be encoded, as can be seen in the "text/plain" encryption type, which converts spaces to + symbols. Another important attribute is action="upload". It makes sure that the data encoded in the form is sent to the "/upload" URL. The input element with the type "file" simply works as a call to the operating system's file dialog, which pops up and lets the user specify the file location. Finally, the input element with the "submit" type deals with sending the request with form data when the button is clicked:

```
<%@ page language="java" contentType="text/html; charset=ISO-8859-1"
    pageEncoding="ISO-8859-1"%>
<!DOCTYPE html PUBLIC "-//W3C//DTD HTML 4.01 Transitional//EN"
    "http://www.w3.org/TR/html4/loose.dtd">
<html>
<head>
<meta http-equiv="Content-Type" content="text/html;
charset=ISO-8859-1">
<title>File Upload</title>
</head>
<body>
<center>
    <h1>File Upload</h1>
```

```
    <form method="post" action="upload"
        enctype="multipart/form-data">
        Select file to upload: <input type="file" name="file"
size="60" /><br />
        <br /> <input type="submit" value="Upload" />
    </form>
</center>
</body>
</html>
```

When pressing the **Submit** button, a stream of bytes is sent to the server, which will forward them to a servlet called Upload. Note that mapping from the /upload URL to the Upload servlet happens in the /src/main/webapp/WEB-INF/web.xml file, as shown in the following lines:

```
<web-app>
  <servlet>
    <servlet-name>Upload</servlet-name>
    <servlet-class>org.javaopencvbook.webapp.UploadServlet</servlet-
class>
  </servlet>
  <servlet-mapping>
    <servlet-name>Upload</servlet-name>
    <url-pattern>/upload</url-pattern>
  </servlet-mapping>
</web-app>
```

Pay attention to the fact that, when the user hits the **Submit** button from the form, the doPost method from the mapped servlet class, UploadServlet, is called. This method is the core of this web application, and we are going to see it in detail in the following code:

```
@Override
protected void doPost(HttpServletRequest request, HttpServletResponse
response)
throws ServletException, IOException {
  System.loadLibrary(Core.NATIVE_LIBRARY_NAME);

  loadCascade();

  Mat image = receiveImage(request);
  Mat overlay = loadOverlayImage();
  detectFaceAndDrawHat(image, overlay);
  writeResponse(response, image);
}
```

The main action in the `doPost` method starts by loading the OpenCV library, as seen in the previous chapters, and then loading the cascade which will be used later for face detection. For the sake of brevity, the initialization is made here, but in actual code, you should use `ServletContextListener` in order to initialize it. Then, the `receiveImage` method deals with receiving bytes from the upload and converting it to an OpenCV matrix. So, the other methods take care of loading the fedora hat image and detecting people's faces so that the overlay can be drawn through the `detectFaceAndDrawHat` method. Finally, the `writeResponse` method answers the request. We will cover `receiveImage` in more detail in the following code:

```
private Mat receiveImage(HttpServletRequest request) throws
IOException, ServletException {
  byte[] encodedImage = receiveImageBytes(request);
  return convertBytesToMatrix(encodedImage);
}
```

Note that `receiveImage` simply grabs bytes from an upload request in `receiveImageBytes` and then converts them to a matrix. The following is the code for `receiveImageBytes`:

```
private byte[] receiveImageBytes(HttpServletRequest request)
throws IOException, ServletException {
  InputStream is = (InputStream) request.getPart("file").
getInputStream();
  BufferedInputStream bin = new BufferedInputStream(is);
  ByteArrayOutputStream buffer = new ByteArrayOutputStream();
  int ch =0;
  while((ch=bin.read())!=-1) {
    buffer.write(ch);
  }
  buffer.flush();
  bin.close();
  byte[] encodedImage = buffer.toByteArray();
  return encodedImage;
}
```

This is the default code to receive an upload. It accesses the "file" field from the form and gets its stream through `request.getPart("file").getInputStream()`. Then, a buffer is created, so all data from the input stream is written through the `write()` method as long as there's data from the upload. The byte array is then returned through the `ByteArrayOutputStream` class's `toByteArray()` method. Since what we have received at this point is just a bunch of bytes, there is a need to decode the image format and convert it to an OpenCV matrix. Fortunately, there's already a method that does that, `imdecode`, from the `Imgcodecs` package, the signature of which is as follows:

```
public static Mat imdecode(Mat buf, int flags)
```

The `buf` argument is a `Mat` buffer that we will create from the byte array, and `flags` is an option used to convert the `Mat` buffer returned to grayscale or color, for instance.

The complete code for the decoding can be seen in the following lines:

```
private Mat convertBytesToMatrix(byte[] encodedImage) {
  Mat encodedMat = new Mat(encodedImage.length,1,CvType.CV_8U);
  encodedMat.put(0, 0,encodedImage);
  Mat image = Imgcodecs.imdecode(encodedMat, Imgcodecs.CV_LOAD_IMAGE_
ANYCOLOR);
  return image;
}
```

Now it's done, we have received the user's image upload, and it is converted to our well-known `Mat` class. It's now time to create the mixed reality.

Image processing

In this section, we are going to describe how to process the received image in order to draw an image file on top of it. Now, a cascade classifier is run just as in the previous chapter. It is important to pay attention to the XML cascade file location. Throughout the code, we have used a helper function called `getResourcePath`, and we have used the convention of storing all the resources in the `src/main/resources/` folder. This way, the helper function works in a manner similar to that of the following code:

```
private String getResourcePath(String path) {
  String absoluteFileName = getClass().getResource(path).getPath();
  absoluteFileName = absoluteFileName.replaceFirst("/", "");
  return absoluteFileName;
}
```

Using this function, one can load a cascade through the following call:

```
private void loadCascade() {
    String cascadePath = getResourcePath("/cascades/lbpcascade_
frontalface.xml");
    faceDetector = new CascadeClassifier(cascadePath);
}
```

After the cascade has been correctly loaded, we are all set, and now it is time to explain how the hat's position is estimated. When running the face classifier, we have a good idea not only of the face's position, but also of the face's bounding rectangle. We will use this width to estimate the width of the hat. We can suppose that the width of the hat would be three times the face's bounding rectangle width. This way, we still need to keep the hat's aspect ratio. This is done with a simple rule of three, as shown here:

$$\text{hat width} = 3 * \text{face width}$$

$$\text{hat height} = \text{hat width} * \frac{\text{original hat height}}{\text{original hat width}}$$

Now that the virtual hat's dimensions are defined, we still need to estimate its location. From a couple of tests, we could infer that 60 percent above the face's bounding rectangle should be fine for most of the pictures. Now, we have the hat's dimensions and position. In the end, instead of using the hat's width as three times the face's width, a value of 2.3 times the face's width seemed to work better. The following code shows the math used to set the **region of interest (ROI)** to draw the fedora as implemented in the method `detectFaceAndDrawHat`. A simple adjustment is made to the hat's dimensions when it goes beyond the bounds.

```
double hatGrowthFactor = 2.3;
int hatWidth = (int) (rect.width *hatGrowthFactor);
int hatHeight = (int) (hatWidth * overlay.height() / overlay.width());
int roiX =  rect.x - (hatWidth-rect.width)/2;
int roiY =  (int) (rect.y  - 0.6*hatHeight);
roiX =  roiX<0 ? 0 : roiX;
roiY = roiY< 0? 0 :roiY;
hatWidth = hatWidth+roiX > image.width() ? image.width() -roiX :
hatWidth;

hatHeight = hatHeight+roiY > image.height() ? image.height() - roiY :
hatHeight;
```

The following screenshot gives us an overview of the widths and the process of drawing the fedora overlay:

It is time to draw the hat! This should be as simple as locating the hat's position in the picture and copying the submatrix. We need to be careful, though, to correctly draw transparent pixels and not draw outside the picture. Mat's `copyTo` method is used to copy a submatrix into another one. This method also accepts a mask Mat parameter, the nonzero elements of which indicate which matrix elements must be copied. Notice that the hat image itself is passed as the mask parameter, and it actually works because all transparent pixels are made zero in all channels and all other pixels will have some value, working like a mask. The code to resize the fedora and copy it to the main image is as follows:

```
Mat resized = new Mat();
Size size = new Size(hatWidth,hatHeight);
Imgproc.resize(overlay,resized, size);
Mat destinationROI = image.submat( roi );
resized.copyTo( destinationROI , resized);
```

The response image

We have successfully received an image and drawn hats over identified faces. Now, it's time to send the result back to the user. We do this by setting the content type of our response as image/jpeg, for instance. We then encode our response with the same format as defined in our header—if it is jpeg, we will encode it in JPEG—and write the bytes in our response servlet object:

```
private void writeResponse(HttpServletResponse response, Mat image)
throws IOException {
  MatOfByte outBuffer = new MatOfByte();
  Imgcodecs.imencode(".jpg", image, outBuffer);

  response.setContentType("image/jpeg");
  ServletOutputStream out;
  out = response.getOutputStream();
  out.write(outBuffer.toArray());
}
```

The input image and the output result appear in the following screenshot. Some fedora hats are distributed to Einstein and his friends in our augmented reality web application. The left-hand side photo is the uploaded image, while the right-hand side photo shows the hats drawn over the detected faces. According to our loop, hats will be drawn in the same order that detected faces are returned. This way, we can't grant a correct Z-order, which is what hat is drawn on top of another although we could try to infer it from face size. This is shown in the following images:

http://www.nobelprize.org/nobel_prizes/physics/laureates/1921/einstein-photo.html

Summary

In this chapter, we sent our computer vision applications to the server-side world. We started covering the basics of a simple servlet-based web application configuration using Maven, which provided us with a general application structure. We then added OpenCV dependencies to our `pom.xml` configuration file as used in a standard OpenCV desktop application. We then checked other runtime configurations as we deployed our web server using Maven.

With every webapp configuration aspect solved, we moved on to the development of our mixed reality application that explored the details of image uploading, converting it to an OpenCV Mat object and then writing a response to our clients with a processed image.

It seems that all aspects of creating basic computer vision applications have been covered now. We dealt with setting up OpenCV for Java and then learned how to work with matrices. We then touched on the basics of creating Java Swing desktop applications and worked with image-processing algorithms to filter, change image morphology, and do essential thresholding. You also learned tools that are in every computer vision researcher's toolkit, such as Hough transformations to find lines and circles as well as special kernel convolution. We covered the important Fourier transform and warp operations. We then dived into machine learning and used handy OpenCV cascades, and you also learned how to create new object classifiers. Besides this, we studied certain background removal approaches and tested the incredible Kinect device to perform depth-based processing. We finally finished the book with a complete server-side example, and now, you are ready to count on Java for your own computer vision projects!

Index

Symbols

2D Kernel Convolution 48

A

AdaBoosting 92-94
affine transformations 77
Ant
  used, for building project 14-17
Apache Ant
  URL 4

B

background subtraction
  about 104, 105
  averaging 106-108
BGR (blue, green, and red) format 30
bilateral filtering 52, 53
boosting theory
  about 91, 92
  AdaBoost 92-94
bucket fill tool 47

C

camera
  video, capturing from 37-40
canny transforms
  and Laplace 73, 74
cascade classifier
  custom cascade classifier, creating 99, 100
  object detection 97, 98
  training 98
  using 96, 97

C/C++ compilers
  URL 3
circle Hough transform
  and line transform 75-77
CMake 2.6
  URL 3
contours
  searching 111-115

D

dependencies, OpenCV
  adding, to web application 130-132
Discrete Adaboost 94
Discrete Cosine Transform (DCT)
  and Discrete Fourier Transform
    (DFT) 71, 79-83
distance transforms 86, 87

E

Eclipse
  Java OpenCV project 7-10
  web application, importing 133, 134

F

face tracking 91
files
  images, displaying from 32
  images, loading from 32
flood filling 58-62
foreground detection 104
frame
  differencing 105, 106

G

Gentle AdaBoost 94
geometric transform 77-79
Gnu C Compiler (GCC)
  URL 3
gradients
  and sobel derivatives 72

H

Haar-like features 84
histogram equalization 88, 89

I

image pyramids 62-64
images
  displaying, from files 32
  displaying, with SwingC++ 33-36
  loading, from files 32
  processing 139-141
  uploading 136-139
integral images 83-85

J

Java Developer Kit (JDK)
  URL 4
Java development
  OpenCV, getting for 2
Java Native Interface (JNI) 2, 29
Java OpenCV Maven configuration 17
Java OpenCV Maven project
  pointing to Packt repository, creating 24
Java OpenCV project
  in Eclipse 7-10
  simple application 13, 14
Java Virtual Machine (JVM) 2

K

Kinect
  about 103, 116
  application, creating 123-125

drivers, setting up 118, 119
features 117
OpenCV support 120-123
setting up 118
URL, for drivers 118
Kinect Motor 119

L

Laplace
  and canny transforms 73, 74
line transform
  and circle Hough transform 75-77
Local Binary Patterns (LBP) 96
LogitBoost 94

M

matrix manipulation 27-29
Maven-based web application
  creating 128-130
median filtering 51
mixed reality web applications 135
Mixture of Gaussians model (MOG)
  about 109
  using 110
morphological operations 53-58

N

NetBeans
  configuring 10-13

O

OpenCV
  building, from source code 2-6
  download page, URL 3
  getting, for Java development 2
  support, for Kinect 120-123
  Swing GUIs, integrating with 42-44
  URL 7
OpenCV SourceForge repository
  URL 2
OpenNI
  URL 118

P

Packt repository, pointing to
Java OpenCV Maven project, creating 24
Windows Java OpenCV Maven project,
creating 17-23
pixel manipulation 30, 31
process 104
project
building, with Ant 14-16
Project Object Model 17
Python 2.6
URL 3

R

Real AdaBoost 94
region of interest (ROI) 140
response image
writing, for web application 141, 142

S

smoothing
about 48
averaging 48-50
bilateral filtering 52, 53
Gaussian 50, 51
median filtering 51
sobel derivatives
and gradients 72
SwingC++
used, for displaying image 33-36
Swing GUIs
integrating, with OpenCV 42-44

T

thresholding 65-68

V

video
capturing, from camera 37-40
playback 41
VideoProcessor 104
Viola-Jones detector 96

W

web application
executing 132, 133
image, processing 139-141
image, uploading 136-139
importing, to Eclipse 133, 134
Maven-based web application,
creating 128-130
OpenCV dependencies, adding 130-132
response image, writing 141, 142
setting up 127, 128
Windows Java OpenCV Maven project
pointing to Packt repository, creating 17-23

Thank you for buying
OpenCV 3.0 Computer Vision with Java

About Packt Publishing

Packt, pronounced 'packed', published its first book, *Mastering phpMyAdmin for Effective MySQL Management*, in April 2004, and subsequently continued to specialize in publishing highly focused books on specific technologies and solutions.

Our books and publications share the experiences of your fellow IT professionals in adapting and customizing today's systems, applications, and frameworks. Our solution-based books give you the knowledge and power to customize the software and technologies you're using to get the job done. Packt books are more specific and less general than the IT books you have seen in the past. Our unique business model allows us to bring you more focused information, giving you more of what you need to know, and less of what you don't.

Packt is a modern yet unique publishing company that focuses on producing quality, cutting-edge books for communities of developers, administrators, and newbies alike. For more information, please visit our website at www.packtpub.com.

About Packt Open Source

In 2010, Packt launched two new brands, Packt Open Source and Packt Enterprise, in order to continue its focus on specialization. This book is part of the Packt Open Source brand, home to books published on software built around open source licenses, and offering information to anybody from advanced developers to budding web designers. The Open Source brand also runs Packt's Open Source Royalty Scheme, by which Packt gives a royalty to each open source project about whose software a book is sold.

Writing for Packt

We welcome all inquiries from people who are interested in authoring. Book proposals should be sent to author@packtpub.com. If your book idea is still at an early stage and you would like to discuss it first before writing a formal book proposal, then please contact us; one of our commissioning editors will get in touch with you.

We're not just looking for published authors; if you have strong technical skills but no writing experience, our experienced editors can help you develop a writing career, or simply get some additional reward for your expertise.

Instant OpenCV Starter

ISBN: 978-1-78216-881-2   Paperback: 56 pages

Get started with OpenCV using practical, hands-on projects

1. Learn something new in an Instant!
   A short, fast, focused guide delivering immediate results.

2. Step by step installation of OpenCV in Windows and Linux.

3. Examples and code based on real-life implementation of OpenCV to help the reader understand the importance of this technology.

4. Codes and algorithms with detailed explanations.

Instant OpenCV for iOS

ISBN: 978-1-78216-384-8   Paperback: 96 pages

Learn how to build real-time computer vision applications for the iOS platform using the OpenCV library

1. Learn something new in an Instant!
   A short, fast, focused guide delivering immediate results.

2. Build and run your OpenCV code on iOS.

3. Become familiar with iOS fundamentals and make your application interact with the GUI, camera, and gallery.

4. Build your library of computer vision effects, including photo and video filters.

Please check **www.PacktPub.com** for information on our titles